THE PURF

THE PURPLE REVOLUTION

THE YEAR THAT CHANGED EVERYTHING

NIGEL FARAGE

Biteback Publishing

First published in Great Britain in 2015 by
Biteback Publishing Ltd
Westminster Tower
3 Albert Embankment
London SE1 7SP
Copyright © Nigel Farage 2015

ISBN 978-1-84954-863-2

10 9 8 7 6 5 4 3 2

A CIP catalogue record for this book is available from the British Library.

Set in Adobe Garamond Pro

Printed and bound in Great Britain by
CPI Group (UK) Ltd, Croydon CR0 4YY

To my long-suffering family

CONTENTS

CHAPTER 1

EUROPEAN ELECTIONS: MAKING BRITISH POLITICAL HISTORY

ALMOST CHOKED ON my bacon sandwich. And it's not often that a Liberal Democrat can make me do that.

Would I, Nick Clegg asked on the Nick Ferrari LBC radio programme, be prepared to face him in a live television debate to talk about the European question?

It was an odd request for a political leader whose Liberal Democrat Party was facing electoral wipe-out in the European and local elections of May 2014, less than three months away.

1

'Let me think about it,' I said.

I delayed giving an answer for a few reasons. The first was that I could not quite work out Clegg's motives. It marked a big risk for him given that the Liberal Democrats were – according to the polls – looking set to be devastated in the May European elections.

The second reason was that, even with my chutzpah, I was nervous. I have been on BBC *Question Time* and Radio 4's *Any Questions* countless times – both of them risky forums; a foot wrong and you pay dearly for it – but a live television debate was a whole new ball game. I really couldn't afford to mess this up. Also, to be fair to Clegg – whom I have known for years from when he was an MEP in Brussels – he was declared the best debater in the country after the live debates between himself, Brown and Cameron in the run-up to the 2010 general election.

Having been an MEP since 1999, I had delivered speeches on the floor of the European Parliament in Brussels, but never something this big. And I was apprehensive. Also, to delay announcing my decision was more dramatic. So I said I would announce my decision on the same radio programme where Clegg had laid down the gauntlet: the Nick Ferrari show on LBC. It created a bit of speculation in the media: was I too chicken to do it? – that sort of thing. On the show, Nick prodded me. I teased him for a bit. 'What d'you think I should do, Nick?' I asked. Of course, I then accepted the challenge on air.

The live television debates were a big risk. Ever since I had returned as leader of UKIP in 2010, I had set down winning the European and local elections in May 2014 as a marker. I had told party donors, UKIP activists and the press – in fact, anyone who would listen – that we had a good chance of winning them.

In Europe, 350 million people have the vote to choose MEPs who represent them in Brussels. UKIP was putting up candidates for every MEP constituency in Britain. The May elections also allowed Britons to vote for local councillors up and down the country. If UKIP could beat Labour, the Conservatives and the Liberal Democrats in both sets of elections, we would be on our way. We would be able to show that we were not just a protest party that retired colonels from the Shires voted for. If we won, we would be able to prove for the first time that we had broad appeal, that we could take votes from the traditional Labour working class, and from moderate, middle-class Tories. It was our chance to show that we replaced the Liberal Democrats as the third force in British politics, and to give the establishment in Westminster a bloody nose. Politically, and financially, UKIP could not afford to mess this up; I would spend the whole party coffers on winning these elections – by polling day, we had just £6,000 left.

As soon as I took the debate challenge, Patrick O'Flynn, the UKIP head of communications, and Alex Phillips, my media aide, swiftly started negotiations with Liberal Democrat central office. The Liberal Democrats were pretty helpful and played a straight bat with us, which I hadn't expected. LBC were to host the first debate and, to my astonishment, the BBC agreed to do a second debate between the two of us a week later.

The original dates offered were 27 March and 3 April. The debates would be just over a month before people across the EU were due to go to the ballot box to vote for MEPs and local council members.

April 3rd happened to be my fiftieth birthday, so I rejected it out of hand. I didn't want to spend my birthday standing next to Clegg, no offence. So I suggested the 2nd instead.

The format – agreed between us and the Lib Dems – was pretty straightforward. We each would present a short argument summarising our position on Britain's relationship with the EU and then Ferrari would select a question tabled by a member of the audience whom LBC and the BBC had chosen to represent both sides of the debate. We would not know the questions beforehand. Clegg and I were both given a minute for each answer with a large stopwatch visible to us. The whole debate would be shown live and then there would be a YouGov opinion poll immediately afterwards.

Patrick O'Flynn and Gawain Towler, whom I hired in Brussels ten years ago to work for UKIP, started drafting some of the issues that we expected would come up and arguments that I could make. I have never been one to make notes, let alone write a speech. In 2013, I wrote my party conference leader speech and it was a mistake. I was far too leaden. I am much better with a clear head, thinking on my toes. But both Patrick and Gawain impressed on me as we rehearsed various questions and answers that, no matter how well prepped I might be, once I was on that platform I was on my own. I also recognised that the questions suggested had to be selected by LBC and the BBC, so they would be sensible ones.

On the evening of the first debate, the media coverage ahead of it was getting bigger and bigger. It had been a strange day. Malaysian Airlines flight MH370 had mysteriously disappeared a few weeks before, and despite the story of the missing jet still dominating the news agenda for the day, the media focus on that evening's debate just kept growing. The debate was scheduled for 7 p.m., and I left the UKIP office in Brooks Mews, Mayfair early. Traffic in central London is so appalling it's difficult being on time anywhere if you drive. The venue for the debate was a corporate hotel on Northumberland Avenue, just off Trafalgar Square. We were so early I decided to go via the Westminster Arms for a quick pint, much to the total astonishment of everyone in there.

Then off to the Britannia. As we pulled up outside the rather corporate hotel, I could scarcely believe the scenes in front of the entrance. There was a mob of photographers and cameramen. At that moment, I did just think to myself: 'What the hell are you doing here, Nigel? This is far bigger than anything you have ever done before. What on earth have you done this time?' Call it a profusely English trait, but I am pretty good at not showing my nerves – but blimey, I was nervous.

We were shown into a separate ante-room. And then straight onto the platform.

Clegg opened the debate. He is certainly no fool and is pretty polished. He kicked off by playing the 'fear card'. If we leave Europe, he said, we cut ourselves off from being a part of a union that makes us stronger, safer and richer. If we pull out, we run the risk of not being able to recover from the financial crisis. It was a bit woolly.

Then it was my turn. Imagine, I said, that you are being asked to join the EU rather than extricate yourself from it. Would you join a club that charges £55 million a day as a membership fee? Would you sign up to a club that would impose thousands of new laws over which neither your own Parliament, nor you, have any say? And would you sign up to a club that would open your borders to 485 million people who can live in your country, bring their families and do as they wish?

The questions from the audience were well chosen – why hadn't the British public been given a referendum? Were there benefits to migration from Eastern Europe?

The debate was pretty straightforward and quite clean. But I regretted that my answers were heavy, a bit too serious, and maybe hectoring. I should have been lighter, injected a bit of humour, but, largely, I was OK with it.

As soon as we left the stage, YouGov started polling to see who was deemed to have won the debate.

It says everything about the media and the political class that in the so-called spin room after the debate it was universally agreed that Clegg had won it hands down. Most political journalists in the UK – called lobby journalists – work as a pack. There are a few notable exceptions but in the main they are feral. While few of their readers (or editors) realise it, they agree between themselves what the story is, what 'line' they are going to take. That way no one ever is surprised by a call from a night news editor revealing that they have missed a big scoop. The press may be free in this country, but little of it is independent. Regardless, the media and the Lib Dems thought that Clegg had come out of it best.

I didn't know, but left to go to a fund-raising do at the Reform Club, the palatial club on Pall Mall, just down the road from the Britannia. I had told the Kipper donors that I couldn't make it for the start but would join them for a drink later. I could have walked to the Reform Club – it is such a short distance – but I really didn't want to be mobbed by reporters. As I got in the Land Rover, Gawain called me: 'Polls are in, Nigel. You're comfortably in the lead.'

57 per cent of those polled thought that I had won the debate, whereas 36 per cent said they believed that Clegg had. YouGov had polled about 1,000 people.

At the drinks at the Reform Club, I knew that I really had to focus hard on the next week's debate. Clegg, wounded by the poll, would come back harder and probably better in the second debate. In all the years that I have known Clegg in Brussels and Strasbourg and all the events where I've bumped into him, I cannot recall a single interesting anecdote about the man. Not one. But while he may be a bit dull, he is certainly not stupid and I knew he would try much harder to beat me the following week.

I also realised that I was at a massive disadvantage to the likes of Clegg. As with all of these things. No other party leader has my diary. No other party leader organises his own diary for that matter. I don't let anyone near mine. UKIP simply doesn't have resources like the Tories, Labour or the Liberals. We don't have the infrastructure of staff and so much of the job of overseeing the day-to-day running of UKIP falls on my lap. I help handle relations with donors, strategy of the party, most of the press coverage – and I'm also an MEP. Life was and remains utterly frantic.

Of all the times that I have done *Question Time*, which was probably the nearest I had got to doing a live television debate, I don't recall ever doing it when I felt well, or having any energy. The amount of travelling I do between London and Brussels just wears you out. Clegg, who is just under three years younger than me, looks much more fresh-faced, and no wonder. He even has time to do the school run, for goodness sake. Watching the first debate afterwards,

I realised that I looked tired and sweat more than Clegg under the lights.

So, with that in mind, I spent the next five days off the booze, I took some long country walks near the house in Downe – in my job I rarely have time to exercise – went to the steam room a few times and had some early nights. Normally, I go to bed at about 1 a.m. and then up at 5 a.m. or so. I was determined not to feel and look like a wreck in the next debate. I wanted to be in the position for once in my life where I did not feel completely shattered.

On the morning of the second debate, 2 April, we briefed the *Daily Telegraph* that my plan for the evening was to attack Clegg on how he had been a political insider all his life, citing his lobbying career in Brussels, and arguing that he had vested interests in the continuation of the European Union. I am proud of how Patrick O'Flynn called this right. By leaking that, it meant that Clegg would have to spend the day preparing to be the aggressor in the debate. This tends to play out very badly with British voters. The British electorate do not like to watch two politicians slug it out – it's not theatre, as some of the boorish MPs in the Commons believe, it just looks ugly and undignified. Aggression also suggests desperation.

We reached Broadcasting House, this time not via the Westminster Arms, and went into the BBC Radio Theatre. David Dimbleby was hosting the second debate, as he had done in 1975. He had said that, forty years on, the topics being debated on Britain and Europe were nearly exactly the same – democracy and jobs. His job, he said, was to get me and Clegg debating.

From the minute we kicked off, Clegg was on the attack, throwing verbal punches everywhere. He seemed cross and frustrated. He was under pressure and it showed. There are things, he said, that are so big, like terrorism, that you can't fight them on your own. For the first ten minutes, I really was on my heels – not on my toes – and he was coming out with some clearly prepared lines – Britain would become Billy No Mates, and then Billy No Jobs. Clegg also used a pre-rehearsed joke which bombed: he said that the Liberal Democrats were the party of 'in' and UKIP was the party of 'Putin'. It was a bit contrived.

I waited – Patrick and I had talked about our strategy

for the debate. Let him attack for as long as he could; it turns the voters off and makes him look like he believes he is on the back foot. I remember looking at him and thinking pretty early on in the debate: 'He's got nothing left. He has no more bullets.'

I tried to keep my cool, to come across as relaxed and to be lighter, less hectoring than in the first debate. I dealt with the arguments, was non-aggressive and just matter of fact.

One of the best questions was about the strain that immigration had put on Britain's local services – GP surgeries, schools, housing.

I was able to remind the audience that the then Labour government had predicted just 13,000 Eastern Europeans would come to the UK and that Clegg had written in *The Guardian* newspaper that the influx to Britain would represent a 'wee trickle'.

In fact, I pointed out, the increase in net migration has been, and continues to be, so vast that Britain cannot plan anything because we have no control over the numbers of EU migrants coming over our borders. Local authorities have no idea how many extra primary school places we will need, and GP surgeries have no idea how many new patients will be trying to register.

At the end, Dimbleby gave both me and Clegg the opportunity to sum up each of our arguments. I looked straight into the camera and urged viewers to join our 'People's Army' and help us bring down the political establishment. It was the first time I had used that phrase. I don't know who had come up with it – it might have been me, I can't remember – but it had been kicking around the office. It was, however, to become the mantra of our European election campaign.

At the end of the debate, I offered my hand to Clegg and, reluctantly, he accepted it. We tried to look friendly with each other. I knew I had done well.

Backstage, in the corridor, the two of us rubbed shoulders as we were preparing to leave. 'I suppose you're going to a private club again, now,' Clegg said to me, referring to the last debate when I had raced off to the Reform Club. 'No, Nick, I'm not. But last time I went to the Reform Club, which, unless I am very much mistaken, is the birthplace of the Liberal Party.' I cackled and walked off.

In fact, I was due at a drinks party at Stuart Wheeler's

flat in Mayfair. I say 'flat' but Stuart's London apartment, which he has since sold, is beautiful and large. As I arrived, the atmosphere was euphoric. The party was full of Stuart's friends and Kippers who had been watching the debate on the television in the flat before I arrived.

As the poll results began to come through, they showed that they were dramatically in my favour. Instant polls put me on 69 per cent and Clegg on 31 per cent. Astonishing.

The first person I bumped into at the party was Lord Hesketh, the car-racing fanatic who left the Tories and joined us in 2011. As the polls came in, people were elated. I felt that night that we had really had a chance to talk about borders and trade – that we had grown into a real party with plenty of messages.

We stayed for a few drinks, then me, Patrick O'Flynn and Alex Phillips decided to carry on. I had, after all, been very well behaved on the booze front to prepare for the second debate. We managed to trot round to The Guinea pub, one of my all-time favourites, on Bruton Place. It was quite surreal, standing outside this seventeenth-century pub on a beautiful spring evening with so many people coming up to us and asking about the debates, having my first drinks for five days.

I felt that that night, even though it was 2 April and the European and local elections were just over a month away, was when the campaign really started. The success of the debates had ignited people's interest in the elections, and they had given us a massive boost. I felt we were in a very, very good place. As it turned out, far too good a place. I may as well have stood on a hilltop and said 'Shoot me'. Our early success meant that the Tories would come at us even harder. The last three weeks of the campaign would turn out to be utter agony.

* * *

On 23 April, we launched the UKIP national tour from Sheffield. Why Sheffield? Well, it's a happy coincidence that it's Clegg's constituency, but it was actually because we wanted to promote the idea that UKIP is not a party of traditional Conservative voters, that it attracts a broader vote and that the working classes are welcome with us.

So I travelled up to Sheffield that Tuesday and we launched a nationwide billboard campaign. The billboards were the culmination of around six months' planning with an agency called Family (based in Scotland), Paul Sykes (one of our most loyal donors) and me. We had started thinking of themes and ideas for the billboards even before my back operation the previous November. I signed off on all of them and by the time we got to April, I was thrilled with the ones we chose to go with. The idea for each of them was to get people talking, to engage voters on the whole European issue and to try to encourage them to get out and vote. I hoped they would create a stir. I was not disappointed. The poster of which I was particularly proud showed an escalator going from the shore of the English Channel leading up to the top of the White Cliffs of Dover with the line: 'No border. No control. The EU has opened our border to 4,000 people every week. Take back control of our country. Vote UKIP on 22nd May.' The media went mad, as I suspected they would. I was accused of being racist because the poster campaign revealed the full extent of immigration into the UK.

One poster led with the question: 'Who really runs this

country? 75 per cent of our laws are now made in Brussels.' It seemed that whenever I made the point that more migrants had come to Britain in 2014 than ever before, I was somehow a xenophobe. Even when I stated that we were discriminating against migrants from countries such as India and New Zealand, members of our Commonwealth, to make way for Romanians, this was somehow unpalatable in the wine bars media luvvies frequent in Islington and Shoreditch. Talk about being out of touch with their viewers and readers. A poll at the time of our campaign found that 77 per cent of those surveyed believed that something should be done about immigration levels. Yet I was not allowed to express the view that British workers have been hit hard by the effect of cheap European labour, that the influx of migrants eager to do the same job for less has effectively made the minimum wage the maximum wage. It is ironic that the Labour Party was founded on principles of looking after the interests of the working class, yet Miliband is more than happy to gift control to Brussels.

So began our national tour: public meetings up and down the country to talk to voters about the EU, immigration, education, the health service. Everything that matters. It was also to encourage them to get out and vote on election day. From Sheffield we went to Gateshead, followed by Manchester then Dudley. It was really hard work. In addition to the public meetings, I was doing hours and hours of local media.

The national tour lasted a fortnight. What I found astonishing was that the Tories and Labour were nowhere to be seen. They just didn't bother canvassing or even trying to get the vote out. I suppose that lot are afraid of leaving Westminster. We just kept going, from Portsmouth to Bristol to Swansea to Derby.

The nationwide campaign coincided with our television party political broadcast. I was pleased with it. It laid out some fairly bald and shocking facts about the financial cost of our membership in the EU, and the personal cost to Britons. To meet current levels of immigration in this country, a house would have to be built every seven minutes. Setting up a business in the UK now is fiendishly hard because 3,580 new EU laws have been introduced since 2010 that effect how British firms can conduct themselves. It seemed that no one was allowed to mention the extraordinary strain that immigration levels put on local services, primary schools, GPs and housing.

On Sunday 27 April I was back home, just over three weeks before polling day. I had got back to Downe the night before. I was exhausted and just wanted to see my two girls. Unusually for me, I turned my phone off. When I switched on the television on the Sunday morning, the reports were that UKIP was in the lead in the polls. We were polling at 35 per cent. I was astonished, and scared.

There is only one thing worse than being behind, and it's being in the lead. It is a very vulnerable place to be. I was scared that we had peaked too early and that we had just made ourselves a target. Now that the Tories, Labour and the Lib Dems could see how far ahead we were, they would know that they still had some time to get their acts together, and attack UKIP and me. After I saw the news, I drove to the newsagent's to buy a copy of the *Sunday Times*, which had sponsored the poll. Our semi-detached cottage in Downe is far too remote for newspaper delivery and the days of having a few shops in a village are over. They've all been wiped out by the supermarkets.

So I got in the Volvo and drove to get the papers. I had a deep sense of foreboding, which proved to be prescient. The press were about to go for us with fresh zeal. They were going to have us for dinner. The *Sunday Times* poll triggered a drip-by-drip constant media attack that would last until election day.

The first nightmare concerned a girl called Sanya-Jeet Thandi. I had known her since she was twelve. She comes from a Sikh family in Medway – right in the middle of my south-eastern MEP constituency. I had known her since she was a teenager because she had been at school with my youngest son, and her mother had also taught my boy. In about 2010, I was addressing a public meeting in Gravesend and she was there. She told me she had joined the party and expressed her keenness on the UKIP message. She spoke very well in public and when she applied for an internship in Brussels, we got her one within an MEP's office there. She did six months for us in Brussels. I recall that when she was there I even called her mother and said that Sanya must be made to understand that Brussels is not the safest of places – in truth, it is rough – and that UKIP couldn't be in loco parentis.

I couldn't have done more for her. She was the girlfriend of a well-known Tory political blogger and was studying at the London School of Economics. I was aware at the time that she was under considerable pressure from her peers for being a member of UKIP.

Early on in May, Sanya had appeared on *Channel 4 News* to defend UKIP immigration policy. She argued that Britain had turned its back on the rest of the world and instead had opened its door to migrants from Eastern Europe. As always, the immigration issue is a tense one.

A week after she did Channel 4 – we were just days from polling day – Sanya issued a statement to the press saying that while a member of UKIP she had been subject to racism. I was mystified.

I could not understand why she had said it. I was certain she had not been the victim of racism. She went onto *Channel 4 News* and said that she had resigned from the party because she believed that we reached out to people who supported racism.

It did us real harm.

There was more trouble ahead. This time it would be my

fault. I gave an interview with James O'Brien of LBC. It is clear to me now that I shouldn't have done it.

I knew that as a broadcaster he had been ticked off by Ofcom, the media regulator. It was a pretty hectoring interview. Why did I say that I would be concerned if Romanian men moved in next door? Well, with 28,000 arrests in five years in the Metropolitan area alone ... Why was I a member of the Europe of Freedom and Democracy Group? ... It was boom. Boom. Boom. This was hardly an interview. It was him broadcasting his views. In any case, it was a mistake on my part, and it went down badly. Patrick and I were normally very selective on who we talked to and O'Brien was an example of bad judgement to say the least, on my part.

The interview was done on a Friday and the following day I was at home, catching up on paperwork. I was terribly worried that I had done something in that interview that would change the course of the campaign. It is at times like this when you realise who you can rely on and draw genuine support from. I spoke to Paul Sykes, our biggest donor, about it and he was immensely reassuring. Paul, the Barnsley son of a miner who made millions selling buses and coaches and dealing in property, is pretty no-nonsense and not easily fazed. He was behind the construction of Meadowhall shopping centre in Sheffield and during his career had employed thousands of people. He was one of the few people in whom I could confide.

But, sure enough, as I expected when I went to buy the Sunday papers, they were far from nice. There was less than one week to go to election day and the coverage was appalling. *The Sun* and the *Mail on Sunday* both ran pieces saying how terrible I was talking about Romanians. How dare I? The BBC ran a line about how no Romanians had come to the UK at all. But the very newspapers who were attacking me for expressing concerns about Romanian immigration into the UK ran screaming headlines a few pages later about Romanian gangs involved in child trafficking.

Did my comments on the Friday before election day cost us votes? I'm not sure. But by the weekend, we were already down about 5 per cent in the polls, which then settled at 28 per cent until election day.

Monday morning brought no comfort. Stuart Agnew, the UKIP MEP for eastern England and a Norfolk farmer, had been putting up campaign boards as people shouted abuse at him from their car windows, calling him a racist.

The press campaign managed to turn people who were not naturally in favour of UKIP into people with a hatred of us, fostering a belief that we were somehow a racist organisation. This filtered through to the grass-roots level. Canvassers experienced real unpleasantness when they went campaigning door to door. One UKIP man in north London tried to stop another man from tearing down UKIP posters and got his teeth knocked out. The police pressed no charges. Unbelievable.

But, in a funny way, it did embolden the core part of the UKIP vote. They seemed even more determined than before to get out and vote. What did those miserable few weeks cost us? Without them, perhaps we could have got 15–20 per cent more, but overall we held fast at about 28 per cent – still enough to win and draw blood from the Tories and Labour and decimate the Liberal Democrats.

Just before polling day – that Thursday in May – something strange happened. I remember saying to Patrick O'Flynn, 'This isn't normal. It's gone eerily quiet.' The phone was not ringing. What more could I do? I had travelled the length and breadth of the country already, holding public debates, campaigning. We had invested heavily in the billboard campaign.

But the press coverage we were getting was appalling. By the time polling day arrived on 22 May, it was a huge relief.

Given that they were local and European elections, there wasn't much I could do on that Thursday, sitting in the office in Brooks Mews in Mayfair. So I went for lunch, had a few drinks afterwards and just waited. We had been in the lead for so long, it had been gruelling. It is far more exciting being the horse that comes up on the inside to win than having to keep the pace for three weeks.

We didn't get the proper result through until the following Sunday, when I was in Southampton for the count. By then, the polling was pretty accurate. It was enormously exciting. As the results came in, great swathes of the map of the UK started to go UKIP purple. I was shocked by the results from Wales. On the electoral map, we looked to have almost as much as Plaid Cymru. We topped the poll in Merthyr Tydfil, for goodness sake. We had fought an election campaign in

Wales, of course, but nothing that warranted this sort of result. We just hadn't had the resources to compete with Labour, and certainly there was no real party infrastructure there. So, when the Welsh results started to come in, I was flabbergasted. We got 28.1 per cent of the vote. Labour got 28.7 per cent. I think what UKIP had done in Wales was to remind them what a rotten deal they were getting out of Cardiff when they looked at the health and education provisions Westminster meted out to them under devolved power.

It is strange, I know this from my days in the City, but when you have a huge success, it can leave a very bitter taste in the mouth. When you are sitting on a massive loss – when a trading position just gets worse and worse and you just keep losing more money – it is an enormous relief when you just think, 'Right, to hell with it. I'm getting out of this' and you cut your losses, get out and go for lunch. It's very clean.

It is quite different when you have a trading position and you make a lot of money. Instead of being enormously smug and cheerful at your gain, you start to beat yourself up that you had not got in earlier and made more money. I felt that way about Wales. To be just 0.6 per cent of the vote away from beating Labour. Why on earth hadn't we tried that bit harder? We were so close. Imagine that fool Miliband's face.

The European elections would turn out to be the moment that we made British political history, but as the results were still coming in, I had plenty to be furious about.

The year before, we had deselected a UKIP MEP called Mike Nattrass. At one time, he had been deputy leader of the party. He tried to sue us. It all got very unpleasant. But even though he lost that time, we were to lose in a very different and more damaging way in our battle with him.

Nattrass, who was a very wealthy property man from the West Midlands had, to our incredulity, been allowed to set up his own party by the Electoral Commission. His new party, which was to stand in the May European elections, was to be called 'An Independence from Europe', not a world away from my UK Independence Party. Worse still, because its title began with an 'A', it was at the top of all the ballot papers for the European elections, with its slogan 'UK Independence Now'. Voters have their lives to lead, most do not have the time to make sure that they have studied all the major candidates and would perhaps not suspect that someone with a name and raison d'être purporting to be like UKIP would try to pull the wool over their eyes. Many people saw that party's name and thought it was us. They got a third of a million votes – quite unbelievable. Undeniably, it cost us at least two seats, some think it cost us three. Allowing Nattrass to launch a party with that name was shocking and showed the absolute contempt that the establishment have for us on so many levels. It also meant that they were given the green light to dupe voters.

I was furious. Talk about the status quo – anything that could be done to damage UKIP. I cannot imagine anything similar being allowed to happen to either the Conservatives or Labour.

Nonetheless, despite Natrass and the media campaign to seriously undermine us, we got the biggest proportion of the vote in the EU and UK local elections and we made British political history. It was the first time that any party since 1906 apart from Labour or the Tories had won a national election in Britain. We now had MEPs in every region in Britain. It was seismic. With 4.37 million votes – or 27 per cent – we were the biggest party, and we got twenty-four seats. In the local elections, UKIP gained 161 councillors up and down the country.

What the result proved was that we were capable of bagging real broad appeal. No longer did our policies only resonate with disaffected, traditional Conservative voters, we were getting the Labour working-class vote as well. We had long been pilloried in the press as a protest party whose meetings were dominated by retired colonels who live near Salisbury Plain and are desperate for the reintroduction of the birch and the first pink gin of the day. We have a few of those, but the May results proved without any shadow of a doubt that we were also digging deep into the Labour vote. We were taking votes off the Liberal Democrats too, who got barely 7 per cent of the vote, compared to our 27. They lost ten seats in Brussels, leaving them with just one MEP. That night represented a convulsion in British politics. We were now the third political party in Britain. The Liberals were decimated. What was also extraordinary was that one in five voters in those elections were people who had not voted for anyone in twenty years. We connected with the British public, long disaffected by the ruling political class in Westminster, in a way that Cameron, Miliband and Clegg could only dream of.

I didn't get much sleep that night, maybe an hour or so. Then it was straight from Southampton to London to do the national media. I was exhausted but I couldn't wait. Somewhere in the back of my mind I had been rehearsing this day for years. All the derision, all the sacrifices, all the hard work. Today was about to prove once and for all that it was worth it. There is a world of difference between having the whole political class despise you because they think you are beneath them and having the whole political class despise you because you are a threat. My dream had become a reality.

We were due to hold a press conference at the InterContinental London Westminster, near St James's Park. I had told Patrick to meet me at the Westminster Arms beforehand. The pub – one of my London favourites – is a five-minute walk through the backstreets to the hotel. Besides, I'd been up since 6 a.m., I'd done the *Today* programme and *BBC Breakfast*, and we'd driven up all the way from Southampton. I deserved a pint. The two of us were sitting in the corner, quietly reflecting on what had been a four-year campaign to bring us here – to bring us to making British political history. It seemed a long time ago since I was re-elected as party leader in 2010, when I told anyone who would listen that UKIP could win the European elections of 2014. Most of our supporters were happy that we had ambition, but few believed it was possible. Stuart Wheeler, one of our longest-term donors, I recall very clearly looked at me quite oddly when I predicted as much to him.

No sooner had the Frenchman behind the bar handed me my pint of Kent's Best and we sat down, there were hundreds of photographers outside the pub. It was just surreal.

Throughout the journey from Southampton to London, I had been chewing over what the results meant for us in the general election of 2015. It was clear that the successes we had made in the local elections up and down the country that day would help us draw up the list of target seats we would fight in May 2015 in order to get our first UKIP MPs into the Commons. I knew by then, of course, that we would probably have a few by-elections before May 2015 (of more later), but it was the target list for the general election that was important at that moment. Unlike the vast might, infrastructure and wealth of the Tories and Labour, UKIP simply couldn't afford – in any sense of the word – to fight a national campaign as they do. We needed to focus on key seats, and the local and European election results shone a light on them: Portsmouth, Yarmouth, Boston, Great Grimsby, Plymouth, Aylesbury and Rotherham. Our next test, however, was to be the Newark by-election – nine days away. The Tories had a rock-solid majority there. The euphoria of our European election win would be short-lived: Newark was to teach me some very painful lessons about how woefully under-prepared we were for fighting for Westminster seats.

* * *

The European election result challenged two great perceived wisdoms of the British media: that UKIP was only ever going to be a protest vote and as such would never win a Westminster seat, and that Euroscepticism was the territory of the political right.

For years, most Eurosceptics were on the left of the

political spectrum. It is worth remembering that Oswald Mosley, who had been both a Tory and a Labour politician, was a staunch pro-European. As founder of the British Union of Fascists, he had dreamt of a United States of Europe.

But, in May 2014, the sheer scale of scepticism about the European Union expressed through votes for right-wing parties blew us all away.

When 150 million Europeans turned out to vote, many of them used the ballot box to tell their own governments: Europe isn't working. Across the Continent, Eurosceptic parties were winning massively. Our electoral result triggered a seismic shift in British politics, but the tremors were being felt across Europe. The Europhiles who feed off Brussels always argue that any problem with the European project can be solved by having more Europe – more integration between member states, more laws.

But Brussels could not ignore what voters across the Continent were telling them.

In France, Marine Le Pen's National Front came first with a quarter of the vote. The French Socialists, led by President Hollande, got less than a sixth. The National Front, which has long campaigned to extract France from the euro and to see the end of the European project as a whole, declared that the result was so damaging for President Hollande that he should call for new domestic elections. It was never going to happen, of course, but Marine's demands show how empowered the National Front were by the European elections. The fact that the French had voted in their droves in favour of the National Front was a terrible body blow to the European project. The whole model of a political union across the EU had been cooked up by the French and Germans and for it to be rejected so forcefully by France was very damaging.

The aftershocks of the political earthquake spread beyond the French borders.

The austerity drives in the preceding few years designed to help the Greek, Italian and Spanish economies reduce their debts and set their lands in order after the financial crisis did nothing but fire up Euroscepticism. It is bad enough suffering appalling unemployment, watching your business fail, and seeing the value of your home collapse – as many across Europe experienced after the financial crisis – but to find out that your lot has been made even worse by

Brussels technocrats is hardly going to endear you to the European project.

In Greece, Syriza, a far-left party, got more than a quarter of the vote, beating the incumbent New Democracy Party. In Denmark, Eurosceptics topped the polls.

The big question after the huge Eurosceptic vote was whether the parties – including UKIP – would form an anti-EU alliance. There is a huge incentive for them to do so. If you have enough bulk to form a bloc in Brussels, you get more funding and more clout in EU committees – in short, you can really throw your weight around. Not long after the election result, Marine did a deal with the Northern League in Italy, also Eurosceptics, to join her European Freedom Alliance. The Dutch PVV party (led by Geert Wilders), the Austrian nationalist party (the Freedom Party of Austria) and the Belgian Vlaams Belang Party all joined as well.

Marine was desperate for us to follow suit.

We had had dealings with the Italian Northern League before in previous parliaments, however they had a very extreme wing, and we pledged never to work with them again. One of their MEPs – Mario Borghezio – an appalling man, was convicted of trying to set fire to migrants in Italy, and then made remarks saying that he understood the rationale of Anders Behring Breivik, the far-right Norwegian responsible for killing seventy-seven people in 2011.

When Marine, whom I have since met two or three times, first took over the National Front in 2011, she gave an interview to the *Daily Telegraph*. In it she said that she wanted her party to be like UKIP – not the British National Party. She has certainly made a number of changes since then. She tried to distance the party from its racist, anti-Semitic history when her father led it and, to make it more moderate, even allowing people who had not been members of the party to stand as candidates. The transformation is quite extraordinary – to go from a party whose leader was convicted of anti-Semitism to securing an approval rating of 46 per cent in polls in the autumn of 2014.

But every time she was interviewed she proclaimed that I should get in touch with her and that she would welcome UKIP with open arms into her anti-European alliance. It drove me mad. It was a distraction I didn't need. I had, and have, no intention of joining her.

When she ran for the leadership of the party, she ran against a man called Bruno Gollnisch, a convicted Holocaust denier who quibbled over the number of Jews who had been murdered. Frankly, I couldn't bear to be connected with anything or anyone like that.

My problem was and is not with Marine, who has always been very friendly towards me, but the fact remains that anti-Semitism is in the party's DNA. On each of the occasions I met her, I urged her to ditch the National Front and start afresh. But she will never manage to truly reform the party and shed it of its anti-Semitic past while her father is alive. He is still an MEP and when – even well into his eighties – he is making remarks that Ebola, the horrific virus that has killed 9,000 people to date in West Africa, will solve Europe's immigration policies, she is never going to be able to move on.

The National Front is still a party that is fundamentally about race – the EU is an afterthought.

Geert Wilders, the leader of the anti-Islam Dutch PVV party, is an interesting character, but my real problem with him is that he is always defending the right of freedom of speech, yet he wants to ban the Koran from the Netherlands. That seems pretty inconsistent to me.

However, we did need to form a new group in the European Parliament and I was delighted that we did a deal with Beppe Grillo's Five Star Movement in Italy. They are the first online political party and behind Beppe is the brilliant Gianroberto Casaleggio. The Five Star Movement won 8 million votes in the Italian general election in 2013. They have proved to be a very reliable partner.

CHAPTER 2

DULWICH COLLEGE

AS I NEARED the end of my time in the early 1980s at Dulwich College, the south London public school, I was told by my Careers' Master, after a lengthy interview, that I should aim for a job as an auctioneer.

J. G. Dewes – a former English cricketer who opened the batting for Middlesex in 1947 and for England against Australia in 1951 – must have spotted that I was quite ballsy, probably good on a platform, unafraid of the limelight, a bit noisy and good at selling things.

The traits he spotted in me in the course of the interview couldn't have been more on the money.

Those traits might have made me good in an auction house, but they would also give me the skills needed to be a politician, especially one who would spend the best part of the next thirty years building and selling a new political vision to the British public.

All of those traits were identified, nurtured and promoted while I was at Dulwich College. I owe that school an enormous debt.

To the delight – and surprise – of my parents, I had managed to pass the common entrance exam and was offered a place at Dulwich for the term starting in September 1974.

They were pleased because our family had very strong family links with the school – both my uncles had been there and my father had been to the prep school. My cousin Christopher was already there. My parents might have been chuffed, but their ten-year-old was terrified.

Established in the seventeenth century, it has magnificent gothic buildings among beautiful playing fields – all within a fifteen-minute bus ride into central London. Dulwich

College was designed and built by the same family of architects who built the glorious Palace of Westminster. It is steeped in history and tradition – pride of place as you walk through the front entrance are seven Victoria crosses and one George cross – awarded to old boys of the school from the two world wars.

As you ascend into the Great Hall, portraits of great former pupils hang on the walls, including Sir Ernest Shackleton. On entering the school for the first time, Dulwich was a frightening and intimidating place.

To all intents and purposes, it looked and felt like one of the great classical public-school institutions such as Westminster School or Eton College. But Dulwich was different. During the 1940s, under a Labour government, the college began a scheme called 'the Dulwich Experiment'. The scheme was devised to educate able children from poor backgrounds, where their school fees would be met by the local authorities. It is fitting that the scheme was entirely in keeping with its original foundation in 1619: to educate twelve poor scholars raised in Godliness and good learning.

My first impression of the Dulwich Experiment hit me in my first full year at the school in 1975. The social mix was quite extraordinary. There were boys like me – white, middle class, whose fathers worked in the City – but there was also a huge number of boys who had won scholarships and bursaries covered by the local authorities.

It wasn't just the ethnic mix. Because Dulwich is a south London school with very few boarders, unlike most public schools, it attracted boys from all over London and parts of the south-east.

I remember my first class quite vividly. Sitting on one side of me was the son of the chief executive of a global company, who was enormously rich. They had a huge house in Farnborough Park in Kent, with staff. On the other side of me was a boy who would become a good friend and whose father was a coal merchant in Penge, also in south-east London. It was quite extraordinary.

While the school did stick to its academic traditions, few of the teachers were academics. By the mid-1970s, when I was there, most of the schoolmasters had commanded tanks in the war and wore tweed jackets with leather patches on their elbows. All of them smoked. The rules were that you could not smoke during lessons, but as soon as the bell went for the next lesson, a lit match was straight in the pipe.

One – David Gregory – was an inspirational history teacher who gave me a lifelong interest in the First World War and its battlefields. Another – the then terrifying deputy called Terry Walsh – instilled in all of us boys what he called the eleventh commandment: 'Don't get caught'. He still works at the school in the archives.

Entry to the school was mainly by educational selection but the rules were waived if you were very good at sport. Dulwich did all kinds of sport, from rugby to cricket, and to an extraordinary degree – many distinguished sportsmen taught there; Alan Pascoe, the Olympic hurdler, for one, along with former England Test cricketers. The challenge of the school was to bring out the best in every boy; to find out what you were good at – it did not have to be academic prowess – and nurture what you had as much as possible. It didn't matter if you couldn't translate Latin very well, so long as you could display something you were good at and throw yourself into it. It was this sort of educational model that did not produce a factory line of ready-made Tory MPs, but a range of alumni, from explorers such as Sir Ernest Shackleton to writers like Raymond Chandler and P. G. Wodehouse, from stand-up comics such as Bob Monkhouse to a governor of the Bank of England, Eddie George.

I was good at cricket and golf and loved the CCF (Combined Cadet Force) so much I had seriously contemplated going into the army. Academically, I excelled at history, was keen on economics and was reasonable at English and geography. I was utterly hopeless at everything else. I had no interest whatsoever in science or maths. You had to attain a reasonable standard in those subjects but, beyond the bare minimum, I refused to do anything.

What I did love, however, even from the age of ten, were the lunchtime societies. I got involved in loads of them, from the debating societies to the one for cricket. I absolutely adored the stream of international cricketers who would come and talk to us at the school. Unsurprisingly, I joined the politics society and, because geographically Dulwich is so close to Westminster, we got plenty of Cabinet ministers and MPs coming to talk to us. Backbenchers would hop on the train from Victoria station, ministers would come by car. It felt as if I was in the middle of everything.

By the time I was eighteen I was on the panel, and we invited – and got – great political brains from both the left and the right. What's more, the other students and I got to hear their views at a time of profound change in Britain. We had just had the referendum on Britain in the EEC in 1975 and then the Brixton riots – just down the road from school – in the '80s. I felt I had been given the rarest of opportunities to listen and to talk to both sides of the political divide about everything that dominated the front page of the newspapers each morning. What did Ken Livingstone think about the growth of the National Front? Equally, what consequence did Enoch Powell think would result from the increasing dominance of hard-left unions? Both of them came to speak to us.

It was through that exposure to such big political, and often opposing, figures that I was able to form my own philosophy, my own sense of what worked in government and of what was right.

In 1978, just before Thatcher swept to power, Keith Joseph, whom she had described as one of her closest political allies, came to Dulwich to speak. It was then, in the Great Hall at Dulwich College listening to him, that I converted to the model of economic liberalism that would dominate Thatcherite policy for the next decade. He expressed a vision of free-market conservatism where hard work yielded success and that those who were financially successful should be able to keep more of their own money.

I was acutely aware as a teenager that after the 1974 stock market crash, lawyers, brokers and proffessional people were paying 83 per cent income tax. You could have been forgiven for thinking that Britain in the mid-1970s was more left-wing than Soviet Russia. The Britain that Keith Joseph described was a meritocracy, and that had enormous appeal to me. He promised that if the country's relationships with the unions changed we would be a beacon for investment from around the world. At the age of fourteen, I bought it hook, line and sinker.

My political views over my teenage years were not shaped by what I was taught in the classroom but by the school, which encouraged open debates and views from across the political spectrum. In 1978, I joined the Conservative Party.

What I got from Dulwich was a generally good, all-round education, for which I am extremely grateful. I am still a huge supporter of the school and of what it stands for and go back to speak to the boys fairly regularly. The last time I went there, I managed to leave with the headmaster's watch in my pocket – he, like I, shares the habit of taking his watch off just before speaking, and I picked up the wrong one.

Exactly twenty-five years after me, my eldest son went there. It was in many ways even better for him. The quality of the teaching was much higher – in my day a number of the teachers were terribly good old chaps and they had had a good war, but were hardly cutting-edge teachers.

There is another vital difference. When my son was there, the social mix was entirely different from my day. When Sam reached the sixth form, he was the boy who came from the poorest family by far. When I was at Dulwich, rich families had holiday homes in Salcombe or Cornwall. When Sam was there, rich families had holiday homes with yachts in St Lucia. The change reflected how the professional rich – the lawyers, fund managers and accountants – had become massively, massively richer over the last twenty-five years.

And there was no boy in Sam's year whose father was a coal merchant in Penge because successive governments, after I left, began to take away the local authority grants to pay for able, poor kids to go to Dulwich. The college did try to build its scholarship system up, but could not get the numbers to the previous scale because of the cost. In reality, Dulwich just could not match the sheer volume of money that was coming from the government.

Now, the government spends the same amount of money to send kids to schools where they achieve far less of their true potential. The grants system started to go under the Tories but Labour did nothing to fight for it either.

What I see in the comparative experiences of the school for me and Sam, I see replicated in what happened to British society over the last twenty-five years – a shocking widening of the class system, where the rich have got a lot richer and the poor are robbed of opportunity to attain their best. As a country we are underselling ourselves.

In a recent Ofsted report, it was found that two-thirds of children in the state education system were not achieving their potential.

Dulwich taught me a number of things – the value of a meritocracy, to start with. At school I revelled in the criss-cross of different classes – you mixed and you only got ahead by your own efforts. It was to stand me in good stead when I went into the City. On the metal exchange, the social mix was just as varied: from a handful of Old Etonian drop-outs to barrow boys from the East End, and you only survived on how much money you made.

But Dulwich also taught me how to mix with people. I can genuinely go up to anyone and have a conversation with them regardless of their background. To be fair, the City also helped with that. I look at other politicians and see how awkward they are around people they don't know. The likes of Cameron and Clegg have only ever mixed with a very narrow social strata of society. I think that is also why people find it difficult to pinhole me – am I posh or not? They just don't know.

Having the benefit of a Dulwich schooling really helped form my views on education. Getting rid of the grammar school system was a wicked thing to do; selective schools help kids from poor backgrounds achieve higher levels of attainment. For decades, the grammar school was one of the most effective vehicles of getting poor children out of poverty and making something of themselves. The lack of a state system of selective schools has created a terrible apartheid of those given opportunity and those who only get opportunities if they are extremely lucky. It says a lot that 60 per cent of Britain's gold medal winners in the London 2012 Olympics went to people who were educated privately.

Certainly, as someone with a good secondary education but who didn't go to university, this has underpinned my view that the vast numbers of youngsters who go to university should be reduced. I think academic children should go to university but that Britain should reinstate trade schools. This country seems to have a reverse form of snobbery where 'ologies' are far better than proper trade schools that could teach you how to be an engineer or a chef.

I don't think my political thoughts and ideology have changed radically since leaving Dulwich. For sure, later running my own City business and seeing at first hand how Brussels operates when I became an MEP taught me a good deal about the effects of economic policy and the consequences of our engagement in Europe, but my gut feelings about things haven't really shifted much.

I certainly don't think it is old-fashioned or regressive to change the education system so that Britain could increase its social mobility, and in so doing increase the national wealth. I would like to see every kid in the UK taught properly, to be taught sport, to have someone take an interest in them and help them identify and nurture what they are good at. Exactly the sort of education I had. But the miserable, desperate truth is that a vast number of children have never had anything like those sort of opportunities. I can only imagine what it must be like to have never had a teacher try to fill you with self-confidence, to convince you that you are worth something and that you have something to achieve ahead of you.

I remember visiting Dulwich just after the 2009 European elections. My old headmaster – David Emms – was there. He had long taken the view when I was at school that I was bloody-minded and difficult. He always saw that I was a wind-up merchant and wrote in my leavers' report that the school would never be quite the same without me, in an 'upside-down sort of way'. But he also told me often that he had tremendous confidence in me. That day, visiting the school twenty-five years later, he told me he had voted for me in the 2010 European elections. That meant a lot.

CHAPTER 3

RISK, ME AND THE CITY

I BET THE BANK on the May 2014 European elections. We may have made British political history winning those elections on the night of Sunday 25 May, beating both the Conservatives and Labour, but we were also broke – again. I had spent all the UKIP funds on winning at the ballot box, bar about £6,000.

It was a risk, but it had paid off. Winning those elections gave UKIP proper electoral credibility that we had never had before. Having also bragged that it was within our abilities to win, I would have looked very foolish had we lost.

I love a gamble, I love stacking up the odds, and it has only been through taking enormous risks that the party and I have got to where we are today.

But it was as a commodities trader in the City of London that I learnt how to calculate and assume risk. The considerations and calculations you make sitting in a trading room looking at the price of copper, ascertaining the downside financial risk of a trade is not a wholly different process to working out the political risk of standing in a by-election that you might not win.

Not only did trading in the City help whet my appetite for taking a gamble, it taught me how to get out when the trade started to go wrong, and to brush yourself off when the losses started mounting up.

Straight from leaving school I went into the City, in my father and grandfather's footsteps, and got a job working for a metals trading business.

I spent my days buying and selling aluminium, copper, zinc, lead, nickel and tin. Anything, in fact, that wasn't a precious metal or that had iron in it, and everything that industrialised countries need to make cars and fridges and kit out buildings. In the City, you rarely take delivery of the metal; it is about locking in the price of it so that your client – say, a car manufacturer – can plan his business for the future.

Trading metal can be big money, big risk and a huge amount of fun.

There is the risk that you may not make much money on a trade and the risk that you may lose a small fortune. There's the risk of a massive swing – for or against you – in the market and the risk that your client could default. Working out how to deal with unexpected volatility in the markets is not that dissimilar to having to deal with an out-of-the-blue political crisis, and making sure you are on the right side of it.

One morning in the early 1990s, having been working in the City for a decade, I lost a seven-figure sum of money in the course of a morning on the zinc market. Not a good day, and it was only lunchtime. I was working for Rouse, an old-fashioned City broking house that had been acquired by Credit Lyonnais, the French bank.

Contemplating the sobering loss I had just run up, I grabbed my jacket to head out into Broadgate, with the aim of being less sober while I considered how much money I was down.

'Where do you think you are going?' my boss yelled.

'Out to lunch – but if you want me to take my jacket off again and stay put, I can start losing the same amount this afternoon if you'd rather,' I replied.

A trading room is like warfare. There are hours of doing nothing then it all goes berserk.

It is no coincidence that Stuart Wheeler and I both cut our teeth in the business of derivatives. Stuart – a championship level international poker player – was an enormously patient businessman and played a very long game in the City, just as he has with UKIP. When Stuart set up IG Index, the spread-betting firm, it took twenty-six years before he floated it and made a small fortune. He was sixty-five when he started selling his shares in the business, eventually making £56 million.

Working in the City did not just teach Stuart and I how to manage risk. It taught both of us how to run a business, something that none of my political rivals have ever done. Both Stuart and I have done stuff on our own before; we have both set up our own businesses – him with IG Index and me with Farage Futures, my own trading company that I set up in 1993 – when everyone thought that neither of us would succeed.

Both of us know what it is like to sit down first thing in the morning and look at the balance sheet of yesterday's trading. We both understand the fear of downside risk, the fear of failing, badly, and the personal cost to yourself and your staff.

Unlike Stuart, I missed my chance to make real money. By the time of the massive commodities boom of 2004–08, triggered by the astonishing economic growth of China and India, I was well out of the City, having decided to close my business – which was still profitable – in 2002 and go full time into politics. That boom came at a very difficult time for me and for UKIP and it did lead me to question what on earth I was doing. That said, I could not bear to go back into the City now. The fun has gone, compliance officers rule, and even as I was preparing to leave the markets I was having to fill in such things as 'risk assessments'. It was just not me.

The City I joined on 1 September 1982 was a world away from the City as it is today.

Maclaine Watson & Co. Ltd – a nineteenth-century metals broker – offered me my first job as soon as I had finished my A levels, which were pretty unremarkable.

I had met a man called Bob McPhie, who was managing director of Maclaine Watson, two years earlier, and had asked him about working in the City. At the time, I had been in two minds about whether to follow my father into finance or join the army. McPhie offered me the chance to go into the office for a day to see whether metals trading was for me.

It was a classic Dulwich College outcome. Many Dulwich College boys were being primed, with five days of school a week plus Saturday mornings and three hours of homework a night, to go to Oxford – or Cambridge if they were good at science. Another substantial number of them were being prepared to make an enormous amount of money in the City. I was definitely in the latter category – just a pity I never made that much money. Like my father and grandfather, I wanted to 'do something in the City', but was unsure what. I had no intention of going to university to faff around for three years and just wanted to get on.

After my day in the office after my O levels, Bob McPhie said that if I wanted a job with Maclaine when I had finished my A levels, it was mine for the taking. I was thrilled. I finished my exams, took the summer off for golf and fishing, and started work in September.

Maclaine was owned by what turned out to be the most disreputable company in commodities trading, Drexel Burnham Lambert, whose main figure was Michael Milken, the man on whom Michael Douglas's character is based in the film *Wall Street*. Once one of the biggest investment banks on Wall Street, it went bust in 1990, engulfed in scandal – everything from insider trading to defrauding clients.

But the old-fashioned Maclaine – situated in Winchester House on Old Broad Street, right in the heart of the City – seemed an awfully long way away from Wall Street. The trading room – full of cigarette smoke, smart suit jackets on the backs of chairs and long desks packed with multi-line phones – was close to the London Metals Exchange and to

Coates wine bar, God help us, where we often went at 11.30 in the morning for sharpeners.

That company was a microcosm of what happened in the City from the early 1980s over the next twenty-five years.

When I joined it was a mixture of an old gentleman's club and very aggressive young men; the Green Suit Brigade with white socks who lived in places such as Basildon and Southend – 'Sarf End', as they would say. It was a cross-section of different parts of society. God knows what they made of me. Hugh Le Fanu, who became (and remains) a good friend, was the son of the Serjeant-at-Arms to the Queen. An Old Etonian in the same year as Boris Johnson, and a year above Cameron, he lived at No. 1 Speaker's Corner. I dread to think what the Queen's Guards must have thought of him staggering home drunk every evening. But the vast majority of the men on the trading floor (they were exclusively men in 1982) were from the Essex Marshes. I liked the mix in the City – nobody cared how posh or rough you were; you were rated on how much money you could make. My first job was in the so-called 'back office' processing the transactions, and it was deathly dull. But the magical door of the City had been opened – and I had walked through it.

One of the myths to have emerged from the financial crisis of 2007 is that the City is full of men who make eye-watering amounts of money and do very little. Actually, a huge number of people who work in the City work very long hours, commute in conditions that are frankly Third World, work under an enormous amount of pressure and are forced to live in the most expensive part of the UK. Few earn a fortune and, even now, it is a really hard-working sector.

When I started at Maclaine, the dark 6 a.m. starts were bad. While I was still living at home in Kent with my mother and younger brother, the early commutes from Orpington station to London Bridge were brutal. Especially in the winter. But by the time I ran my own business, Farage Futures, in 1999, I was getting up at 4.45 a.m., which really is early, so that I could get into the office in time to trade the closing hours of Australia and Japan.

I started on £4,000 a year, and after my first year I got paid a bonus of £300 in 1983. I was very chuffed.

My first five years were fantastic fun. When it was busy

you worked hard, when the market was dead you went for lunch.

It was alcoholic like you cannot believe and, frankly, we were pretty amateur. There were terrible cock-ups in the afternoon, contracts bought instead of sold, some were priced wrongly (decimal points and all those zeros can be tricky after a three-hour lunch), the wrong metal bought for the wrong client. When the mistakes came to light, usually the next day, we would just shrug our shoulders and say: 'It happened after lunch.' It still shocks me how many of my contemporaries and friends did not make fifty years old – a combination of stress and booze. Burn-out, as it is known.

But, despite the long-term cost on your health, the lure of a proper lunch in the City was very great. When the markets were quiet, the trading room would just empty. Lunch was Simpson's Tavern – a fabulous eighteenth-century chophouse hidden down an alleyway off Cornhill – which served mixed grills, sausage and mash, bubble and squeak, all washed down with pints of Young's bitter and a bottle or two of red. Or Sweetings – the most charming of fish restaurants near the old Mansion House – which years later I almost ran. No bookings, heaving with smart brokers. Turn up, share dining tables, order your oysters and all that. It was like being back at school – but with money.

On busier days I'd nip out to The Lamb in Leadenhall Market for a few pints of Young's and a roast beef roll. When it was really busy, you didn't go anywhere. In the 1980s things hadn't really changed much since P. G. Wodehouse's book *Psmith in the City*. The character created by Wodehouse – like me, an old boy at Dulwich College – said that people in the City spend their mornings choosing where to go for lunch then their afternoons telling everyone how good it was.

By the time I had my own business in the 1990s, when it was quiet I would tell my staff to go and enjoy themselves. The London metals market shuts at 5 p.m. and New York closes at 7 p.m. After that, we would just start again. On days out with clients, lunch just carried on. When I took my American clients out, lunch was 12 till 12; that's what they liked.

Occasionally, I met up with my father for lunch. He worked for Coni & Covington when I was in the City and latterly – or rather the last fifteen years (he retired in 2010) –

at the very old-fashioned Walker Crips broking house. Like his own father, he just carried on. My father worked opposite a man called Douglas who claimed to have fired the first shell into Germany. Quite extraordinary. My grandfather had been a partner at a broking firm called Blunt, where he worked for forty years.

By the mid-1980s, I became a pretty good trader, broker and market-maker. Traders buy and sell for their own trading house, brokers do so for a client and market-makers are people who are obliged to offer a price to any member of the metals exchange who wants to buy or sell the metals in which they trade. I remember getting in some pretty tight spots – they are high-pressured jobs – and thinking quite a few times: Good grief, where is all this going? If you called the market wrong you could quickly find yourself sitting on a substantial loss. It taught you how to really hold your nerve, as well as admit when you had messed up. They were lessons that I would need for a career in politics.

But the days of old-fashioned broking were about to change beyond all recognition. And not for the better. By the time that Big Bang came along in 1986 the City was on a path that would eventually see overseas players control Britain's biggest industry and ultimately hand over control of it to Brussels.

Big Bang – so called because the transformation it brought to the City was explosive – was a change in the rules that governed how the City did business. Thatcher effectively opened up the City to foreign banks who were allowed to do everything – buy and sell shares for clients, trade for themselves and trade with each other.

What Big Bang actually opened the City up to was newcomers – especially the large American banks such as Goldman Sachs, Morgan Stanley and Credit Suisse, and what they brought with them was a new corporate culture.

In 1986, I moved from Maclaine and started work for a small trading house called Rouse. Even then, the corporate culture was beginning to stifle me. Along with Big Bang came the Financial Services Act of 1986. That piece of legislation introduced a regulatory culture of box-ticking, rather than leaving people with considerable financial expertise to police the City. It was the birth of a culture that would wreak financial devastation to our banking sector two decades later.

Up until 1986, any commodities broker – like me – could

put a brass plaque up outside their front door and declare themselves to be ready for business. You did not have to register with anyone, and there were no examinations to pass. The only thing you couldn't do was take deposits from clients – you needed an agreement with a bank to do that. But you could certainly be an intermediary broker, and there were loads of small broking houses across the City.

Once the Financial Services Act came into being, a lot of businesses closed down. For sure, some of them were wrong 'uns. I recall one that closed its door was called 'Spondoolee Options'!

The act brought in ghastly regulators – all sitting in their offices in Canary Wharf – who were supposed to police the City and make it safer for people to do business. But the vast majority of those regulators (God, I hate those people) had failed in the City – they frankly did not understand what bankers and brokers were up to and certainly didn't have the wherewithal to spot a problem on the financial horizon. The new culture beckoned in massive banks that dominated the market place and the hapless regulators simply couldn't see the wood for the trees.

From 1986, I was asked to produce such things as risk assessments and would just refuse. It was like Health and Safety for derivatives. The whole point of the City is to take and manage risk and I had no intention of filling out a form to tell the compliance department – by then the fastest growing part of the business – how big the risk was. Growing compliance departments changed the whole culture of the City. Apart from monitoring everything, we had to start minding our Ps and Qs. They basically took the fun out of trading. But they also missed the point. While compliance departments were getting me to tick boxes, they failed to concentrate on the fact that a derivatives industry was growing exponentially under their noses, whose products they did not understand and whose risk profile they were oblivious to.

I had had enough of the new compliance culture and decided to do my own thing. Credit Lyonnais and I agreed we would go our separate ways and, in January 1994, I set up Farage Futures, my own trading firm.

I rented a room at a firm called Refco, the biggest futures company in the world, whose headquarters was based in Chicago. I had friends there who knew I was an entrepreneurial character and they agreed for me to base my little company in their premises. I hired five staff whom I liked primarily because none of us really fitted in. Our room was a tolerant zone – when they brought in smoking bans in the office, we just ignored them. We didn't do much speculating, most of the trading was on behalf of clients, and I stipulated that no more than 5 per cent of our overall business should be proprietary trading – where you are trading for your own firm or, as we called it, for 'your own book'.

Between 1994 and 2002, I owned Farage Futures and ran it. It was hard work, getting up at 4.45 a.m. every morning, and involved a huge amount of travelling, mainly to the US. But, for eight years, I had a fantastic time, basically doing my own thing, in my own way. The timing, however, was not great. I didn't make a huge amount of money, though enough to buy semi-detached house in Kent without a mortgage and enough to get my boys – Sam and Tom – through boarding school.

Had I carried on in the City, and held out until 2004 when the commodities boom really took off, there would have been eye-watering sums to be made. My regular clients were and remain terrific friends, and of the people who worked for me then, I still count many as close friends. I had a wonderful time wining and dining them at Lord's and at the races.

This is singularly what career politicians such as Clegg, Cameron and Miliband simply don't understand. They have never had a proper job. They went straight into either being a political researcher at Conservative Party central office or they started off as a SPAD (special adviser to a minister). They have never run a business, they have no grasp at all of what life is like 'out there', of what it means to employ staff who have to pay mortgages, of going through the previous day's profit and loss accounts at 8 a.m. every morning and sometimes realising that, on a bad day, your staff are earning more than you. They have a complete misunderstanding about people who run businesses – they don't realise that the people you employ often end up being like family. They have no comprehension of what it is like to go through bad times with a business – the depressing days when you have to sort out errors and bad debts.

From the very start of setting up Farage Futures, politics began to impinge. Within weeks of starting the firm, I was running in the Eastleigh by-election. I simply could not have gone into politics unless I had run my own company because I just would not have had the time.

By 2002, I decided to close the firm. It was a bear market, its income was going down, but it was still profitable. I closed it in good order; the accountant who wound it up – who, bizarrely, is standing against me in South Thanet for the Tories – thought I was mad to be closing what was a good little company. But I had had enough of the City; it was no longer any fun and I was desperate to get into politics.

On entering the political sphere, I began to realise, to my horror, just how much Whitehall was giving away to Brussels, particularly with regards to the City. It was disastrous. They had no regard for the fact that the City is Britain's biggest industry and provides billions every year in tax to the Treasury. It was madness to allow Brussels to run it.

The tipping point for me was when Britain joined the European Exchange Rate Mechanism (ERM) in 1990. I had watched the great ERM debates and simply assumed that we would follow the Alan Walters side of the argument. Thatcher's economic adviser had argued that the ERM would be a disaster for Britain – to try to hitch the pound to the German deutschmark and keep them trading in the same bracket. They hoped that by aligning our currency to the Germans we would inherit the characteristics that defined the German economy – stable growth and low inflation. But Britain was in a totally different stage in the economic cycle to Germany. We were going into a recession. They weren't. Moreover, Germany is a very different type of economy to us in the larger sense: they are more of a manufacturing-based economy while we are more service-based. We are much more global than Germany in terms of who we trade with and the companies who invest in the UK, whereas Germany is more Eurocentric. In short, we were economically incompatible.

In 1990, when we went into the ERM, I was sitting in the Coates wine bar on Old Broad Street (it's now a Corney and Barrow). It was about 5.30 p.m. and someone ran in and shouted, 'We've just joined the ERM.' I could not believe that we had done something so stupid – and that it was the Conservative Party – *my* party – that had done it. It triggered a huge break with the Tories for me. It was quite clear that the ERM was the first step towards a single currency. I realised the next day that Labour and the Lib Dems had supported it as well and that, therefore, I would never be able to vote for any of them. I became an ERM bore overnight – at the golf club, in the City – I told anyone who would listen what a disastrously stupid decision we had made in joining it.

Suddenly, I became even more interested in the political pages of the newspapers than the business pages. It became increasingly obvious to me that the grip of Jacques Delors – the European Commission president who laid the foundations for a single currency – was becoming very strong. As a result, the British political classes were slowly losing control of our country.

Trading metals made me realise that London is a global trading centre, not a European one. When I picked up the phone on the trading floor, it could just as well be a client from Santiago, Chile on the other end as someone in Frankfurt. I regret the changes to the City culture that globalisation brought – to the fun and the creeping dominance of tedious regulation – but if the City cannot be global in its nature, it will lose out to the likes of Singapore.

Brussels hates the City – the technocrats there would quite happily see the City close down. They hate what they call the Anglo-Saxon model and they cannot see why an interest rate that is right for the UK economy may not be right for Germany or Greece – the reason being that we are simply different countries.

The ERM was just the beginning of the handover of inherited rights to Brussels, and the City knew it.

When Lehman Brothers, the Wall Street bank, went bust at the height of the financial crisis in October 2008, it became crystal clear to me how much control Whitehall had relinquished to Brussels and how the American-style corporate compliance culture had gone some way to partially destroying Britain's biggest industry.

At the time when Northern Rock, the mortgage lender, had to be bailed out, we subsequently learnt that Mervyn King, the then governor of the Bank of England, had to wait for instructions from Brussels. Because we had handed over financial regulation to Brussels, the Bank of England was denied the function of overseeing the British banking industry, for which it had been responsible since 1694.

Would Northern Rock have got as bad as it did had Gordon Brown not stripped the Bank of England of its powers? I strongly argue that had the Bank of England still had oversight of this country's mortgage lenders – instead of that role being given to the fools at the Financial Services Authority, up the road in Canary Wharf – Northern Rock would not have been allowed to over-extend itself in the way that it did. The mortgage lender – in its desperate attempt to be the biggest home loan provider in the country, drastically – and fatally – increased its lending books. By the time the credit crisis came along, they had to go cap in hand to the Bank of England for help. Within a day of the news breaking that the lender needed emergency help, there was a run on the bank – the first in Britain for a century.

It marked a colossal failure in regulation, and it risked bringing the entire banking system down with it.

What these compliance officers also unwittingly introduced was an undermining of the very fabric of Western capitalism. By allowing banks to be 'too big to fail', and bailing them out when they were on the brink of bankruptcy with taxpayer money, they replaced capitalism with large-scale corporatism. Under capitalist rules, if you run your business in such a way that you go bust, you go bust – the government does not come and bail you out. But the big financial corporations, all the banks, are hand in glove with the political class, both in Whitehall and in Brussels.

So who did the regulatory structure – introduced in 1986 – protect in the end? Undoubtedly the institutions who were bailed out. That regulatory regime oversaw the most amount of money lost in the history of capital markets. It did not prevent the massive pensions mis-selling scandal. It did not prevent the collapse of the insurer, Equitable Life.

At the height of the financial crisis in 2008, one of the first things Brussels technocrats did was to urge the European Parliament to pass a resolution so that the commission could introduce legislation to curtail the activities of hedge funds. It was backed lock, stock and barrel by the Tories, largely because of Cameron's pathetic desire to be popular. The new legislation introduced onerous rules on how much capital they had to hold and how they could trade. Funnily enough, there are no hedge funds that count in Belgium. But the London hedge fund industry was enormous, and once part of Britain's vibrant and powerful financial services business. By the time the legislation came in, one in four London-based hedge funds had gone – to Switzerland, to Singapore, anywhere but the UK or the EU.

If ever there was an example of how Brussels bureaucrats, whose interests are not aligned with ours, can fatally damage British business, it was this.

And it is not stopping with hedge funds. London is still a hugely important financial centre but, all of a sudden, the golden goose is not looking as healthy as it once was.

There are new emerging markets such as Hong Kong and Singapore, which are far friendlier to the businesses at which we excel. We have always been brilliant at insurance, but Bermuda is doing rather well at attracting operators in that industry. What now for our foreign exchange businesses and fund management?

By November 2010, the new Conservative-led coalition, through Tory MEPs, voted to transfer control of the City from London to three regulatory EU bodies that now govern banking, financial services and markets. I would meet British regulators on the Eurostar returning from Belgium to London, having just taken their orders from Brussels. It simply beggared belief.

Do I miss the City? On bad days, do I yearn for the adrenalin, the buzz and the camaraderie? I miss what it used to be like. I would loathe it now.

CHAPTER 4

CAR CRASH, PLANE CRASH AND CANCER: SEEING BOTH SIDES OF THE NHS

I HAD BEEN AT work on Boxing Day 1986 because Wall Street was open, so I'd driven into the City. I traded right through to when New York closed, so wasn't clear till gone 9 p.m., at which time I raced back to Kent. In my village – Downe – there are two pubs, but only one was open that Boxing Day night and I was determined to make last orders.

I walked into the Queen's Head and ordered a pint. All of a sudden, an indescribable pain shot through my left-hand side. It was so acute I nearly collapsed. It seemed to go from somewhere near my left kidney, through my abdomen and into my groin. I was in absolute agony. But I tried to grin and bear it and ordered another pint.

Two days went past and I was still in real pain, at which point I realised that something was very badly wrong. It was so bad that, on 28 December, I went to the Accident & Emergency department in Bromley hospital. Several doctors examined me (registrars, locums, all that lot) and they came to the conclusion that I had a testicular torsion – where your testicle gets twisted. I would need an immediate operation, they said, but their operating theatres had closed for the evening, so I would have to be taken by ambulance to Farnborough hospital (which is, incidentally, where I had been born).

Once in Farnborough, whose theatres were open, I was re-examined by another four doctors, and it was pretty painful. An Indian doctor told me that the Bromley doctors had got it wrong: I had an infection. I was to go home and take a heavy dose of antibiotics. I did not need an operation after all.

A few weeks went by and the pain was just as bad. I had managed to make it into work for some of the time but I quickly just got too ill and ended up sitting at home, feeling miserable. All the time, my left testicle was getting markedly larger. After six weeks, I went to see my GP in Biggin Hill, a very elderly chap even then, and I could tell by his face as he examined me that something was very wrong indeed. By this time, I was having genuine difficulty walking. My left testicle was as large as a lemon and rock hard. The doctor immediately arranged for me to see a consultant that day whose clinic finished at 2 p.m. The old-boy GP was very alarmed and persuaded the consultant's office to fit me in at the end of his clinic.

To say that this consultant was disinterested would be an understatement; perhaps he had a round of golf at 2.30 p.m. 'Keep taking the antibiotics,' he preached, and that was that. I, however, was in a terrible state.

I phoned the office and spoke to one of my bosses. He told me that I was covered with private medical insurance and that I should use it and get whatever I was suffering from sorted.

The next day I was sent to see a private GP in the City at a clinic on Garlick Hill, near Mansion House. His name was Dr Solomon and he told me that while he wanted me to have a scan, he thought that what I had could be very serious indeed. I had been alarmed by my GP's swiftness to refer me, but after that no medical professional had taken me seriously. Until now. He made an immediate appointment for me to see a top surgeon called Jerry Gilmore on Harley Street. At the time I had not realised who Gilmore was. He had built his reputation on treating sportsmen for groin injuries. Dr Solomon was astonished I had not had a scan after all this time and he sent me for one that afternoon. Clare, my then girlfriend, who would become my wife, was with me (a nurse herself) and we were both extremely worried. I had the scan, and the radiographer handed me the results. I did not like the look on his face at all. 'You're going to see Mr Gilmore now, aren't you?' he said. 'You're going straight there, aren't you, not stopping at the pub on the way, are you?' Bloody hell. I went to see Gilmore.

He examined me and looked at the scan. Very quickly he came to the conclusion that I had a tumour in my left testicle and, there was no doubt about it, they were going to have to remove the testicle. There was to be no debate about it and it had to be done soon.

I was not happy about this at all. It doesn't matter how much people tell you that you have two, I certainly didn't want one of them removed, and definitely not at the tender age of twenty-one.

I was referred to the Princess Grace hospital at the back of Marylebone. On the day of the operation, Clare and I took the train from Kent into London, then got a cab. As soon as we arrived at the hospital, I was asked to sign a consent form. The two of us were properly scared, terrified in fact. I tried to make a joke and asked them to make sure they got the correct testicle. But it was all horrendous. They shaved me and drew a big cross on the ball that was soon to be no more.

As I came round, the anaesthetist came in to talk to me and I knew from his face that everything was far from alright. He stared at me and said, 'They can do marvellous things these days,' and with that, turned around and walked out. It was like something out of a film. Quite surreal.

Neither Clare nor I had prepared ourselves for what was about to happen next. Gilmore entered the room and said that I had cancer, and that he believed, due to the results of bloods they had taken, it was almost inconceivable that I would not have secondary tumours in my stomach and lungs. I was terrified. It makes me upset even now – thirty-odd years later – to think about it. There I was, a 21-year-old, being told that I was almost certainly riddled with cancerous tumours.

The cancer they had found in my left testicle was a blood-born tumour, which was why Gilmore was convinced it had shot through my organs so fast. I was never very good at science at Dulwich College, but it's funny how the language of a diagnosis, which would normally mean nothing to you, stays with you for life. Before that day in the Princess Grace hospital, the phrase 'Alpha-fetoprotein' would have meant nothing. It did now. It related, Gilmore said, to a type of blood count. A high reading, as it was then, meant more tumours; a low one: life.

It was astonishing. For the best part of two months I had been fobbed off by one NHS doctor to the next – apart from my GP, all the rest thought I had nothing more serious than a common cold. All they had had to do in that first night in the A&E department was to have me referred for a scan.

This time, at the Princess Grace, I was to be sent for a full CAT scan to see where the cancer had chosen to set up home. CAT scans themselves are scary and claustrophobic, especially in the state of mind I was in at the time.

When I came back from the scan, my close friend Hugh Le Fanu, who worked with me in the City, was sitting in my room waiting for me. He had poured us both large scotches.

I remember feeling the most profound sense of fury, that my cancer was just so unfair. For two and a half days, I just thought: 'This is going to be it.' At just twenty-one years old, I had so much I wanted to do, so much I was sure in my mind I was going to achieve. And I was in love with Clare.

That feeling of fury was so overwhelming. I don't know whether every cancer sufferer feels the same way, whether you are twenty-one, forty-one or eighty-one. But I certainly did. The effect on my family was astonishing. It is only now, at the age of fifty and as a father of four, that I realise how my own parents must have felt. Years later a friend told me, and I agree (with my two sons and two daughters), that my diagnosis was worse for my parents than for me.

After the seemingly endless two and a half days that followed, I was due for the scan results. The oncologist – a bespectacled, owl-like man who could have been cast as a professor in the *Harry Potter* films – came to my room. This time it was my turn to shock the doctors. I could tell from his face that he could not believe what was in front of him. I had a fag going (in those days you could get away with smoking in a private hospital room), *Channel 4 Racing* on the telly and I had a few bets on the go. This man – Peter Harper – looked at me with a mixture of wonderment and disbelief.

He told me that, despite the odds, the cancer that had taken up residence in my left testicle had not spread.

After an experience like this, he remarked, some people spend the rest of their life on carrot juice; some go the other way. Eyeing me knowingly, with the horse racing on in the background and a full ashtray on my hospital bed-side table, Harper said that he suspected that I would fall into the latter category.

Because I was so young, Harper, who is now a good friend, said that he was loath to commit me to a course of chemotherapy because it would have made me sterile. Instead, he said that the course of action would be much more cruel. Chemotherapy, he said, was unpleasant, but most people just grit their teeth and get on with it. I was to be given what felt like a six-month sentence. Twice a week I was to go to the London Bridge private hospital and have blood tests. If, in any one of those tests, the protein count went up, I was to be rushed into a course of chemotherapy. The London Bridge hospital – with which I was to form a life-long relationship – was amazing. My commuter train from Orpington in Kent went into London Bridge station and the hospital made sure that my blood tests were scheduled for 8 a.m. every time so that I could work with as little disruption as possible. After the tests twice a week, they became once a month, then every six months. But they didn't get any easier. I hated them. There wasn't a morning of one of those visits when I didn't wonder whether I should be packing a toothbrush.

The cancer – and I am scared of tempting fate – has, to date, left me alone. It has not come back. I'm not sure how it fully affected me, but it has left me with a clear belief that without private healthcare I would probably be dead. I just do not understand that, for want of a scan, I might not be here now. How can so many doctors come to the conclusion that a scan is not cheaper in the medium to long term than being in hospital for three or four days?

For sure, I had cancer thirty years ago, but I have strong views that what I experienced of the NHS then is still the case now.

I left the private London Bridge hospital with a clear view that the NHS is so over-stretched that if you can afford private healthcare, you should take it, particularly for things such as diagnostics and preventative medicine. On the NHS, the system is so battered and poorly run that unless you are really lucky, you will fall through the cracks.

I had discovered just a few years before when I was hit by a car and almost lost my lower left leg, the true value of the NHS: it is astonishingly good at critical care. Unfortunately for me, I would also find new evidence to support its brilliance twenty-five years later, after my plane crash.

But what testicular cancer taught me is that the NHS will probably let you down if you need screening, fast diagnosis and an operation at a time that suits you.

I know how sacred the NHS is to the people of Britain; everyone is scared that it will be taken away from them. But the cost of that fear is that the political classes are terrified of even criticising it. The standard of debate about the NHS on programmes such as *Question Time* is risible. No one – whether Tory, Labour or Liberal Democrat – will say anything other than praising the doctors and nurses of the NHS. Then they get a round of applause and that is it. It is as if you cannot support something and criticise it at the same time.

I have now had three near-death experiences and I've seen the best and worst of the NHS. As such, I am better qualified to criticise and defend the NHS than most politicians.

The real elephant in the room on health is the effect of an expanding population in Britain. No one dares to mention it. No one from any of the main three parties will talk about how the NHS is so over-stretched due to the massive increase in the number of people arriving at our shores. When I went to Boston in Lincolnshire for the 2013 local elections, the average waiting time in Accident & Emergency was between eight and nine hours. Why? Could it possibly be something to do with the fact that the local population had grown by 25 per cent in the few years before? Local services just couldn't keep pace. Immigration has an impact and it is foolish to pretend that it doesn't.

Westminster and the national press – who sing from the same hymn sheet – went spare when I dared to mention that anyone, from anywhere in the world, who can get into the UK, is entitled to an AIDS test, paid for by the NHS, and, if found to be HIV positive, will be given the vastly expensive anti-virals – for free. Health tourism costs us £2 billion a year. But because the Terrence Higgins Trust, the massive HIV charity, lobbied Samantha Cameron so successfully, we are treating any foreigner with HIV, courtesy of the British taxpayer. The press were up in arms. When I dared to mention that our foreign aid budget to places such as Pakistan is close to £1 billion and that the combined cost of military intervention in Iraq, Afghanistan and Libya had put indescribable pressure on our own budget, I was pilloried. But after my comments on HIV tourism, a poll showed that there was real sympathy among the British public in support of my views. I simply do not think it unreasonable to draw the conclusion that charity begins at home – it is the National Health Service, not the International Health Service. We are struggling to pay for the health service we have without allowing new members of the European Union – many of them from very poor countries such as Romania – to benefit from a free hip operation. It would be fine if the number of Britons choosing to have medical treatment abroad in the EU equalled the number who were coming here – but it doesn't. How many Britons would choose to go to Romania for cancer treatment? Migrants and tourists should be made to have health insurance as a condition of entry to the UK.

With our increasing and ageing population, the NHS budget is never going to come down. But, good grief, it could be much better run. Our treatment for conditions such as strokes, heart disease and cancer is behind France.

It is frankly outrageous that since good old Tony Blair came to power in 1997, the NHS has seen a 47 per cent increase in middle management. Fifty-one per cent of all NHS employees have no clinical training – they are administrators, cleaners and the like. It beggars belief. It is deeply ironic that Labour is so evangelical about the need to protect the NHS, because it was Blair who did untold damage to it. The current crisis for Accident & Emergency departments is a direct consequence of the fact that New Labour gave a massive increase in pay to GPs, and simultaneously allowed them to have reduced hours. Not just a shorter working day, but no home or weekend visits. Where are you supposed to go for health-care if you have a sick child with a raging temperature on a Saturday night? A&E, presumably, which is stretched to the limit. The massive outsourcing of contracts, particularly for services such as cleaning, have left us poorer as a result. I cannot help taking the view that the NHS was better run in the 1960s, where the state controlled it outright and we had matrons running the wards. It was Labour's vision to build bright, shiny new hospitals across the country, delivered through private finance initiatives. We certainly got them. The trouble was that the £50 billion cost of building them ballooned to a disastrous £300 billion overhang owed to the private sector when you factor in interest and capital payback. None of this is ever discussed by the political classes – there is no debate or criticism countenanced.

There are huge problems with the NHS, deep structural ones, but, as I have said, I know more than most what that means on a personal level. I know what horror would be brought on the British public, the majority of whom rely on it for all their healthcare needs, if it stopped doing what it is brilliant at – critical care.

For sure, when I had cancer, the incompetence and the negligence of the NHS almost killed me, but it has also saved my life, twice. I am certainly not taking any flak from gutless politicians who claim that I am no fan or supporter of the NHS.

The first time the NHS saved my life was on 25 November 1985. I had been out for a curry, had bored the world and his wife about the Anglo-Irish agreement, drank steadily

throughout the afternoon, and went home from Orpington train station. I did not see the car that hit me, but I was
tossed into the air and landed on my head. Apart from the
head injuries, the damage to my lower left leg was so severe
I was told that I could have lost it altogether. Even now, I
have a thick lump of bone sticking out. I was in casts for
the best part of a year – so when the casts came off the following October, it was the first time in eleven months that
I could have a bath. The recovery was miserable, traction
and its series of pulleys is pretty medieval, but the treatment I received saved my left leg. It put paid to any more
rounds of golf, but the nurse who treated me, I married. A
cliché, but not only did I get my life back, I got a wife and
two fantastic sons.

Twenty-five years later, I would again need the NHS
– badly.

*   *   *

I have never been keen on flying. But when, in May 2010,
I stood against John Bercow, the Speaker of the Commons,

for his seat in Buckingham, I thought it would be a bit different if, on election day, I commissioned a small aircraft to fly round the constituency pulling a UKIP banner behind it. It would cost a couple of grand and it would get us some publicity. Banners are a well-known advertising tool used by everyone from zoos to shopping centres. I didn't know the pilot; Justin Adams ran a banner-flying service and he had come recommended by a member of UKIP in Southampton.

So, I resolved to do it. We had a dry run before election day and it was fine, if a little nerve-wracking. To start with, the plane – a Polish Wilgar – was so small that in the cockpit Justin and I brushed shoulders. There was no space for any passengers behind – it was like sitting in the front of an old Mini.

Secondly, the business of attaching a banner to the plane is a complex one. The hook for the banner was suspended on a kind of stilt, and the plane – after taking off – had to swoop down to connect the body of the plane to the hook, thus attaching the banner behind. It took a few goes, but the dummy run went well. I decided to give it a go.

On the morning of the general election, it was overcast. I drove to the grass airstrip myself from home and my press man Duncan Barkes followed in his own car behind.

I had hoped to time the flight – the banner read 'Vote for your country, Vote UKIP' – with the school run and early morning commuters on their way to work. The plan was to fly around the constituency for an hour in the morning and an hour in the afternoon.

From the minute that flight took off, everything was wrong. I knew what to expect from our dummy run when we had picked the banner up on the second try. This time, we missed the third, and the fourth.

When Justin managed to hook the banner, within seconds he said: 'This is an emergency.' I was stunned. He barely spoke but managed to tell me, quickly, that one of the banner's ropes had wrapped around the tail of the plane. These banners are heavy things – they need to be to withstand the wind speed. I knew that Justin was now unable to drop the banner before landing and that we were headed for a nasty crash.

Justin made a mayday call. Not what you wanted to hear just after breakfast.

Justin, now soaking with sweat down his face and neck, was struggling to keep control of the plane. He briefly told me that he was going to gain some height and arch in a circle to return to the airstrip.

I reasoned that he did not want to die any more than me, so I sat in my seat and literally did nothing. I said nothing. As a non-pilot, there was nothing I could do to make any difference to the situation. But my mind was racing. I thought about speaking to him, but would that just distract him? And besides, what would I say?

I thought about making a phone call to my wife, or sending texts to my family. But would that be even worse for them? To have some chilling message from their father on their mobile phone from beyond the grave? So, for the first time in my life, I was in a crisis and I just sat there, doing nothing, scared.

For a few minutes we ascended, Justin turned and it was clear we were heading for the little grassy airstrip. It was also clear to me, and I'm certain to Justin, that we weren't going to reach it.

Increasingly, Justin was losing control of the plane. And

we were coming down quickly. We managed to clear a tiny hamlet and the plane began to lurch from side to side. The ground began to rush up quickly and there were hedges in front of us. Justin and I said nothing to each other.

I remember thinking: So this is it. This is how it ends. When people say that their life flashed before them when they thought they were about to die, it is rubbish. All I could think of was how much I still wanted to do and the impact my death would have on others – my girls were still so little and the boys were only just finding their way in the world. It was a grim reality.

The ground was still rushing up very quickly; the green fields of Brackley in Northamptonshire were very close and we were approaching at a slight incline.

I imagined there would be a loud bang and then everything would go black and then that would be it. It didn't seem that bad.

As the banner touched the ground, the plane became so unstable it nose-dived from about 38 feet, according to the accident report. We hit the ground nose first and then there was this huge noise, which I can still hear to this day, followed by an appalling silence. But I could see light. I remember thinking: I'm not dead. Except being aware that there was daylight, I couldn't see anything. My nose was about six inches from the grass, and I was suspended upside down in my seat, held by my seat belt. Had it been six more inches, it would have broken my neck.

Suddenly, I could smell fuel and I began to feel terrified that I would burn to death. I could hear Justin call for me, but I couldn't reply – I could barely breathe. I managed to wiggle my feet.

With that, I could hear Duncan, who had rushed to the crash site: 'Are you alright?' I believe my language may have been quite colourful, but the gist of it was: 'Get me out of this thing.' I had no idea how to unbuckle the seat belt; it was Duncan who did so, climbing in, and I dropped out. He managed to break my fall to the ground. I grabbed the upturned wheel of the plane to pull myself up and managed to stumble away from the plane for about 15 yards. Then I just sat on the grass. I could taste the blood that was streaming from my split lip and I knew from how much difficulty I was having getting my breath that I must have broken a lot at the top half of my body. I was right.

Sitting on the grass, I didn't feel too good, but I didn't feel that bad either. This, I reckoned, was as good as it was going to get, being able to walk away from a plane crash. I told Duncan to light me a fag. Not a great idea so close to a pool of aviation fuel. I took one drag and felt sick.

I didn't see Justin. Even though the plane was so small, it had thrown us apart. The impact of the crash had effectively ejected the engine of the plane away from the main body, which I think is the only reason that we did not catch fire. Justin, it would turn out, needed to be cut out of the metal of the plane by the fire service. Both Duncan and a man – who I later discovered was a cyclist who had biked over to help – could not get Justin out.

An ambulance arrived, and I was driven to Banbury hospital. I felt every single bump on the way there, I can tell you.

As I arrived at the Accident & Emergency department, it was like something out of an episode of *Casualty*. A full team awaited my arrival. I had numerous hands on me, my clothes were cut from me, and they even provided a beautiful Dutch nurse to hold my hand. She felt like an angel.

I had got a wife out of my first near-death accident and now the NHS provided me with an angelic Dutchwoman for my third.

The scans and X-rays started and it was found that I had fractured two vertebrae in my neck, split my sternum and broken pretty much all of my ribs. Something along the way had punctured my lung. And not forgetting the split lip.

They stitched my lip then and there, but said that the bruising to my heart meant that I was at risk of a heart attack. I was then taken by ambulance to Oxford's John Radcliffe hospital.

As I was wheeled from the ambulance, it was then that I saw Kirsten.

She had found out about the accident when a member of staff at UKIP called her on her mobile. She had been at a school mothers' get-together when she was told of the crash, and then, of course, they put the television on. The television news was already broadcasting pictures of me trapped upside down in the plane. It was a dreadful thing for her to see.

Justin, it turned out, was less hurt than me, but he was still very badly cut and had bled heavily. But he wasn't smashed up. Unlike me, he was taken straight to the John Radcliffe hospital, and, from there, medically we went our separate ways. His sister called me to ask how I was doing and to tell me about Justin.

Very soon after I was admitted to the John Radcliffe, air accident investigators came to see me, and advised me, for legal reasons, that while they carried out their inquiry I shouldn't speak to him. It would be some time before I would speak to Justin again, in even more catastrophic, and frightening, circumstances.

At the time, I remember feeling terribly emotional. How could I have been so lucky?

But, when I returned home – there is little that doctors can do with broken ribs and a split sternum except give them time to heal themselves – it takes a long time for bones to heal and I was in a lot of pain.

Slowly, my poor ribs and sternum began to heal. But the cracked vertebrae – the C5 and C6 that sit in the base of your neck – got progressively worse. My back and neck area had never been great anyway but the plane crash made everything massively worse. When you get to my age, there is always going to be wear and tear, but the car crash in my twenties and the plane crash in my forties left me with a body that was twenty years older.

Just after my recuperation, a strange thing happened. A UKIP activist got in touch with me to say that he had met the cyclist who had stopped on the morning of my plane crash to help Duncan pull me out of the wreckage. He told the Kipper that he was bitter that I had never got in touch with him to thank him and that he put it down to me being a typical politician. It was strange and deeply hurtful. Strange that they should have bumped into each other, and hurtful that he would have thought that of me. Until the activist got in touch, I never knew the cyclist's name – after sitting on the grass I was whisked to Banbury hospital in an ambulance. Once I had his name, I wrote to him and sent him some wine, but I never heard back. Apart from anything it made me realise how much I would despise becoming 'a typical politician' and all the hateful baggage that that would bring – the lack of genuineness, the lack of integrity and the sense that you are just in it for yourself.

My neck injury was not the only consequence of the plane crash that I had to deal with.

From various third-hand accounts, I learnt that Justin, the pilot, had recovered physically but was mentally in a bad way. The day that the aviation authorities published their report in November, I was doing *Question Time* in Maidstone. He rang me. He was very, very drunk. I said to him that the report was great news. It had absolved him personally of any responsibility for the crash. The authorities ruled that it was an accident. He was extremely angry with me and very bitter, and he accused me of selling the story for large sums of money and of cutting him out. He was a hero for landing a plane that had killed neither of us and I was the villain. He had been advised, he said, to go to a Sunday newspaper to give his side of the story about what a terrible person I had been. It was a horrible conversation with a man who, clearly, apart from being drunk, was extremely distressed.

I had never sold a story about the plane crash, nor made

any money from it at all. We were both just victims of an aviation accident.

I asked where he was staying and whether I could go and see him the following day. Having split from his wife and small child, he was living in a village in Oxfordshire where, from what I could gather, he was being cared for. So, with very mixed feelings and a good deal of apprehension, I drove from Kent to the village the next morning.

When I arrived he looked the same as when I had first met him, but this time he was clearly very disturbed, very bitter and very angry.

As we began to talk, it was clear that he had been wound up very professionally by some pretty ruthless UKIP detractors on the internet in conjunction with a journalist at the *Sunday Times*. I was left in no doubt that Justin had been driven mad by a fanatic and a journalist who kept telling him how much I had profited from the crash.

As well as having to recover from his physical injuries, Justin had had to face the stress of the aviation inquiry, from which he was ultimately absolved. But he blamed the length of the inquiry for the split from his wife, and now that he was under the care of the Oxford mental health authorities, who knew of our meeting, he was not able to fly. He had also said that until he was cleared in the inquiry, he could not make an insurance claim for the ruined plane and he had lost his business as a result. He had lost pretty much everything. Both the crash and, ultimately I, had ruined his life.

We spoke for some time and then he said that he planned for us to go to his local pub for lunch. It was a few hundred yards away and we would be met there by someone from the Oxford mental health authorities.

I felt very uncomfortable about going there with him. I was half in mind to just get in the car and drive off. Nevertheless, we met the mental health worker in the pub car park and ordered lunch.

As we sipped our drinks and the lunch arrived, Justin told me that it had been his plan to kill me but that now that I had at least come to see him he had decided against it. All this said in front of the mental health worker, who sat there mute. He had not, he said, ruled out killing me in the future. Justin also told me he had been in the special forces and that he had access to weapons.

I tried to talk to him rationally and point out the positives. He had been absolved of responsibility for the plane crash, I said, so he could claim for the financial loss of the plane and start again. But, with mental health issues that were known to the authorities, I realised he could never fly again.

The three of us finished lunch. By this stage, I was trying to put a brave face on. Would he suddenly pull a knife on me in the car park? He didn't, but he did tell me he was having a pistol delivered to his home the following Monday and that he planned to hunt me down and kill me with it.

As I drove back to Kent, churning the last twelve hours through my mind, I called my secretary and told her what had happened. She had all along implored me not to meet Justin. While I had had no contact with him since the crash, she had maintained contact with him over the phone and had become increasingly alarmed by his behaviour. Then I called my wife, whose view was that I shouldn't have agreed to meet up with him at all.

When I got home, I called the *Sunday Times* and asked to be put through to the editor's secretary. The editor did not take the call. I left a message explaining that one of his reporters was endangering my life and asked him to call me back. He never did.

I didn't know what to do and racked my brains to think of who would. David Davis, the Tory MP, was one of the few members of the political class I liked and whose judgement I trusted. Under both Michael Howard and David Cameron, he had been shadow Home Secretary, and I felt sure that on a matter of safety such as this, his advice was worth hearing.

David heard me out and started off by saying that most politicians – particularly high-profile ones – get personal threats. But he said that this was different. Because it was so specific in its nature, I must go to the police. I took his advice. I made a few preliminary calls to the Metropolitan Police, who set up an interview at Bromley police station the following Saturday morning, which was closer to my home. I spent the morning there.

The following evening I learnt that Justin had been

arrested. I don't whether he had turned himself in or whether the police used my statement as a reason to arrest him. Why he was not sectioned the day I met him with the Oxford mental health worker is beyond me. He was charged with five counts of making threats to kill and was kept in custody until the trial at Oxford Crown Court in April 2011. Apart from providing a character witness for a publican at a magistrates' court, I had never been to court before.

I was cross-examined. I realised that the job of the defence counsel was to deconstruct my argument, so I began to ask him questions. The judge intervened: 'No, Mr Farage. He asks the questions, not you,' he scolded me.

Justin was found guilty and sentenced to eight months in custody but, because he had already served eight awaiting trial, the judge said he was free to go. He was subject to a restraining order.

The whole miserable episode made me reflect even more about the state of healthcare in our country. While the trial was going on, I looked up how many mental health patients kill. It turned out that at the time there were about 120 people murdered each year. I was extremely grateful not be one of them. I found the complete failure of Oxford mental health authorities to do anything, their failure to seek to have him sectioned when he was threatening to murder me in front them, quite frankly astonishing.

As time went by after the trial, I thought about him less and less. A few months later, in November, I was told that he had been found dead in his flat in Eastbourne, having taken an overdose. A desperately sad end.

✳ ✳ ✳

Justin's death did not bring to a close the fall-out from the plane crash. For me, there was more misery to come.

The same month that Justin died I was driving in the Volvo from home in Kent to Brixton in south London and back. On the journey, I lost all feeling in my right arm and hand and couldn't use it at all to steer. The pain in my neck was so acute I was finding it difficult to concentrate.

I called my brilliant osteopath – a Mr Gupta in Gillingham. He agreed to see me the next morning. He is a realist. He told me that there was nothing he could do about my arm, which he suspected had gone completely numb from nerve damage near my broken vertebrae. He told me that I had now reached the stage where I would have to have surgery.

A private MRI scan followed at the London Bridge hospital, and I was referred to a Mr Bhupal Chitnavis, a top-dollar consultant neurosurgeon there. I had seen him before, a month after the crash, but I had deteriorated badly since then. This did not seem to worry Bhupal, an Indian migrant who grew up in Slough. He is incredibly pro-British and, when I turned up in his consulting rooms at the London Bridge hospital and I could barely stand up, all he wanted to do was ask me about UKIP. There was a queue of people in the waiting room outside but he just kept bombarding me with questions – extraordinary. When he did get to talk to me about the scan results from my neck, the news was pretty grim.

He said he was shocked by the damage to my neck and that, if I wanted, he would sign me off as being partially disabled for the rest of my life. I did not voice it, but thought in fairly colourful terms that he could forget that. I certainly did not want one of those blue badges – it would be conceding defeat – but it was a shocking moment. I realised then that I really was smashed up.

He offered surgery. The operation would involve removing both of the discs and, forgive the lack of medical terminology, grinding them up, putting them in new metal discs and returning them to my neck. The operation would last two and a half hours and I would be out of action for at least six weeks. He suggested that I come in the following morning.

I thought hard about this. There were all sorts of considerations. There was the risk that it could go wrong, that the nerves would not heal and that I would be even more 'disabled' than I already was.

But I knew that Bhupal was one of the best, so was less anxious about that than what shape I would be in for the European elections the following May, just six months away. I knew we had a good chance of winning them and that the campaign would be one of the most important things I would ever do in my life. Physically though, would I be up to it?

There was another thing to consider. My neck injury aside, my general state of health was dire. I had done weeks of lunches and dinners for fund-raising and, apart from the appalling pain I was in, I had been eating badly and drinking too much.

So I said no. I resolved to delay the operation for a week and spend the time in between preparing for what was going to be a major operation. I cut out the booze, ate more healthily, slept more and tried to do a bit of walking. I knew that I had to be mentally and physically prepared for this. It was not dissimilar to the preparation techniques I used in the run-up to the second television debate before the European elections the following year.

Bhupal described me as the worst patient of his career. If the operation went well, he would be hailed as a brilliant surgeon; if it made everything worse, everyone would know and his reputation would be ruined.

My operation was scheduled for 17 November. The only upside to this was that the Ashes were due to start less than a week later, so I would be having some serious television viewing time while I was recuperating. If all went well, I would be in on the Tuesday, operated on the same day and home for the following Saturday.

I did not advertise my operation – a few people at UKIP who had to know, knew, as did the main donors. Close friends knew, of course, but, for security reasons – the London Bridge hospital is brilliant at this sort of thing – the name on my door and at the front desk reception was Mr Ali.

So, I arrived on the Tuesday morning and just after lunch, I was taken down to theatre. What amazes me was that they cut through the side of my throat for the surgery, and to this day there is no scar. I suppose the days of stitching have been overtaken to some extent by glueing things back together.

The operation – which is called a radical discectomy – took about three hours. By midnight, I was awake and feeling groggy. And I was desperate for a fag. I instructed the nurse to remove the drain and put a bit more bandage on and said I wanted some fresh air – with that I managed to potter down to the front of the hospital and light my fag. London was dead, it was beautifully freezing and I was alive, drawing on a Rothman's. I felt very lucky.

Within a couple of days, I began to feel better. But that didn't last long.

The painkillers were giving me hallucinations. I was on

three lots of them, including tramadol and diazepam. I would close my eyes when friends and family came to see me and realise that I had no idea what I, or they, had said. It was horrible.

I did try to learn a lesson from the plane crash though. Six weeks after the accident, I had been back on the floor of the European Parliament attacking Barroso. It was too soon and it was absolute lunacy. This time, I knew I would have to cancel loads of stuff in the diary up to Christmas. I had been due to speak at the Lord's Taverners in Lancaster Gate. That had to go. After nerve surgery, bizarre things happen. At first, I could barely pick up a cup of tea. My first physiotherapy appointment was on Christmas Eve. I managed, in a blur, to get through Christmas, and resolved for New Year that I would get off the painkillers, which were robbing me of the ability to think clearly and were still giving me disturbing hallucinations.

As of now, the feeling in my right hand and arm has come back. But I am still in pain and I have some very bad days – not helped, of course, by sitting for hours in the back of a Land Rover, travelling up and down the country. I have a shaped cushion to support my neck, but I have no time to exercise, which also doesn't help. But broadly, the operation was a success – fingers crossed.

Having nearly died three times, I think the effect of the car crash in my twenties, surviving testicular cancer and the plane accident have made me a much bigger risk-taker than I would have been otherwise. When you think your life is about to be taken away from you and you are given it back, you just want to get on and do things. There's no time to waste: children to bring up, elections to win, pheasants to pluck, wine to drink. I think that all three of the near-death experiences went some way to explaining, to me at least, why I gave up what was a good career in the City. It had been going well and, had I hung on, I would have been trading during the massive commodities boom fuelled by the growth of the Indian and Chinese economies. I was well placed to make my fortune. So why didn't I? Why did I give up all of that for a political party that no one had heard of? I feel sure that, had I kept my business going in the City, I wouldn't be living in a modest semi-detached house in Kent and driving an ageing Volvo estate. And my study would not be a shed – albeit quite a large one – at the bottom of the garden.

I was far more shaped by the car crash in my twenties than the plane accident. I resolved then that I just didn't have time to waste and that I really needed to achieve something important – more important than earning money.

There were a few other consequences of these experiences. I still suffer from tinnitus, nowhere near as bad as when I had my car crash, but it is there and it's annoying. I cannot play a round of golf any more, thanks to the car crash – a brain injury can affect your inner ear and it is astonishing how that can damage your hand–eye co-ordination. It's a shame because I loved golf from when I was at Dulwich College and had been quite good at it, in an amateur way. The other, perhaps unsurprising, consequence is that I am even more scared of flying. But there's no real option when I go to the States. I'd love to go on the *QE2* but that isn't going to happen. So there we are. At least I am still here.

CHAPTER 5

BEING AN MEP AND MY GROWING CONTEMPT FOR BRUSSELS

I T WAS JUNE 1999, and I had just been elected as an MEP for the south-east constituency of England for UKIP.

There were three of us – me for the south-east, Jeffrey Titford for the east of England, and Michael Holmes for the south-west.

We walked into the building of the European Parliament – which we had never even visited – and looked at each other in shock. What on earth?

I was just thirty-five years old. One marriage was behind me; Kirsten and I would marry later that year; I had my two boys and a metals trading business in the City that still made money but on which I was spending less and less time.

We had no idea where to start.

The European Parliament building in Brussels is an enormous, utterly soulless warren of offices, committee rooms and bars. Given that it's supposed to represent the 500 million citizens of the EU, in all their diversity, it is a bland cliff of a building that says nothing about everything. Britain was just one star on their EU flag.

From the look of it, it could be a 1960s hospital in the north of England, but far bigger and with far less use. I don't think the EU Parliament has ever saved anyone's life either.

I have always thought that it takes several years once you join an institution to figure out how it works and what you need to do within it, and my early years as an MEP were no exception. The three of us were really quite lost at the beginning.

What I did do early on was to make contact with a veteran Danish Eurosceptic called Jens-Peter Bonde. Through him, we managed to tag onto a group in the European Parliament who were left-wing Eurosceptics. Our association with him in 1999 is a real sign of how the Eurosceptic movement in Europe and the UK has changed: namely, it used to be the business of the left; now it seems to have been completely absorbed by the right – a point often forgotten these days.

We arrived in a momentous year: 1999 was the year that the euro was effectively born. While it didn't come into circulation for another three years, it was then that it became a real currency.

At the time, there were very few critical voices about the euro, monetary union or political union. Anyone who expressed scepticism was considered to be very much marginalised, and certainly not to be taken seriously. No one who was anti-monetary union was perceived as a threat, more as a somewhat mildly entertaining oddball.

Brussels was full of European fantasists then, and when they expressed any kind of zeal for monetary union, they were really talking about political union. They wanted the whole lot – economic union was simply the first step. Even though Blair, with such a pro-EU agenda, had buckled to both Rupert Murdoch and Sir James Goldsmith, the billionaire Eurosceptic, and agreed that he would not dump the pound and adopt the euro without a referendum, Britain had ceded plenty to Brussels by the time I arrived. No one really believed that there would be a referendum anyway. By 1999, in many ways, I had arrived too late – Britain had already given so much away. And it was abundantly clear to me, not just as a British MEP, but as a broker who still had a business in the City, how much Brussels controlled.

They called it integration, but what it was in practice was Whitehall giving away – without any authority from the British people – our inherited rights and freedoms to a bunch of unelected, unaccountable technocrats in Brussels.

Even before the introduction of the euro currency, when I arrived in Brussels, we had given up our sovereign rights for anything that involved other EU countries. Trade agreements, the setting of tariffs, VAT and our agricultural policy were all dictated by Brussels. We signed up to various financial directives that governed how we should police our own capital markets – the second biggest in the world after Wall

Street. For goodness sake, the City – the broking houses, investment banks, private client businesses, commodity traders and hedge funds – contributed 20 per cent of all of Britain's tax revenues. We are world leaders in the business of making money through capital markets; it goes to pay for our hospitals, schools, roads – the lot. Yet the British political class gifted control of it to Brussels without so much as a by-your-leave.

Whitehall just swallowed it. There was no debate in London about whether monetary union, or even EU membership, was a good idea. The Conservative Party during that period played the 'Keep the pound' card, primarily to make themselves distinct from euro-mad Labour. Those were the days when William Hague, former leader of the Tory Party, still defined himself as a Eurosceptic.

I knew, and it proved to be true, that monetary union was only the beginning. It was to be the thin edge of the wedge. Brussels would increasingly seek to control more of our industry, regulate it more and, as a result, drive it away. Brussels hates the Anglo-Saxon practices of the City and, once it got its claws in, it began to bombard Britain's financial services industry with a blizzard of compliance and red tape. In the wake of the financial crisis of 2008, the EU needed to show that it was doing something; they needed to identify a culprit for the banking crisis. The EU Parliament voted to legislate hedge funds, and Labour, the Liberal Democrats and the Tories were all in favour. When the Alternative Investment Funds Directive came into being in 2010, one in four hedge funds left London. It just goes to show how quickly a government can alienate an entire industry, and it mattered not a jot to the EU – we were a global centre for hedge funds; they had comparatively nothing.

My first five years in Brussels were hardly momentous. I got to know the interminable EU system – which would prove invaluable later – and I achieved a few bits and pieces such as fishing. Nothing of which I was particularly proud.

In 2002, I chose to close Farage Futures, my commodities trading business in the City, because I was spending so much time working in Brussels and trying to build UKIP.

Much of my first three years as an MEP was spent travelling the length and breadth of Britain – hosting public debates in town halls up and down the country on the euro, what being a member of the EU meant and what we were giving up to Brussels.

It was also spent trying to deal with the parlous state of UKIP.

In 2000, two of the party's three MEPs – Jeffrey Titford and I – proposed a motion, at an extraordinary general meeting for UKIP at Methodist Central Hall in Westminster, of no confidence in the party leader – Michael Holmes. We succeeded and Jeffrey took over as leader in a bid to try to calm the party, which was at the time riven by arguments and in-fighting.

Jeffrey and I decided that our main focus was to try to build the party's structure across the country and to regain order, and to that end we toured the UK extensively.

2002 was the year that changed everything. Jeffrey Titford decided to stand aside as party leader and Roger Knapman ran to succeed him. We had previously agreed that if Roger won, I would take control of the 2004 European elections. I formed a national campaign committee and started working with donors to draw up a proper fund to fight Labour and the Tories. I was also in charge of selecting candidates and helping to prep them. It was my job to run the administration and planning of the election campaign. The role also meant that I was much more prominent in the public eye than Roger.

In the spring of 2004 (the elections were in June), the Earl of Bradford, who would stand for the West Midlands region and lose, introduced me to Robert Kilroy-Silk, the former television presenter. I felt positive about Kilroy-Silk, who would go on to win the MEP seat for the East Midlands. He would, I thought, raise our profile and help on the campaign trail.

We were gaining traction. We even got Blair to pledge in the Commons in the April of that year that he would hold a referendum on the EU constitution. For sure, the details were pretty thin – there was no pledge on a date (and there never would be) – but at least he was forced into a U-turn.

But, nonetheless, I began to feel ahead of the EU elections that we were making a bit of an impact. In the June elections, we got twelve MEP seats and 3 per cent of the vote in the local elections, held at the same time, across the UK, which put us third, ahead of the Liberal Democrats.

We doubled our vote in London and got our first council seat there. It was marvellous.

When we returned after the elections, we returned as a real party, not a handful of MEPs. Overnight, I went from being an obscure backbencher to being co-chairman of a Eurosceptic group. Rather than being delegated to make speeches on the floor of the European Parliament at ten to midnight when everyone else had left, I got to speak when the house was packed, when commissioners were there and all the rest of it. It was a breakthrough moment – I finally felt that it had been worth leaving the City and that changing careers was beginning to pay off, even though, financially, it certainly wasn't worth it. By 2004, I had three children and was getting considerably worse off, having to re-mortgage the house in Downe. I still have a mortgage now, albeit a small one, but that would have certainly been paid off had I stayed in the City – we could have even moved to a bigger house.

Being an MEP was not conducive to paying the school fees for my two boys and, later, two daughters. My youngest girl was born the following year.

The year of 2004 was pretty full on, and I was spending much of it on the road. It was sixteen days a month in Brussels, where I would just stay in hotels, and one day a month in Strasbourg, which is an absolute pain to get to. There were no direct flights from London to Strasbourg so I would just drive – eight hours solid from my home in Kent. I also spent a lot of time trying to build up the party infrastructure in the south-east.

MEPs can live a life of absolute Riley in Brussels. I think I refused about nine out of ten of the lunches I was offered there. With 15,000 lobbyists in Brussels, all eager to buy influence off you, you could, and many MEPs do, effectively live for free there. Talk about a gravy train. Indeed, you could certainly be taken out for lunch and dinner every day, and pack your afternoons with endless champagne receptions. Some MEPs can get extremely wealthy on the fat of the EU calf. Along with not having to pay for anything, an MEP gets an allowance of €300 a day to spend on nothing.

I rarely went to lobbyist dos – partly because I hated them all and I suspect many of them hated me. Also, the champagne would have been warm and, quite frankly, I have always preferred to be in the pub with my own friends than having to make tedious conversation with a lobbyist.

Other MEPs were amazed at this: that I actually liked spending time with the people in my own office – everyone from researchers to other Kippers. We would take the trainees – or *stagiaires* as they are called in Brussels – to the pub along with our own MEPs. It certainly wasn't the done thing to fraternise and they were pretty surprised at our down-to-earth approach, shall we say. Some MEPs are so grand, they insist on exercising their right to being picked up in a chauffeur-driven Mercedes, ferried around and having the car door opened for them. I mean, really. Who do they think they are?

Europeans can be quite puritanical about how much they think the English drink. But nowhere is there more boozing than in Brussels – by all nationalities alike.

The city functions by being awash with booze. And UKIP was no exception. Our watering hole was, among others, the Kitty O'Shea Irish pub opposite the EU Parliament building on Boulevard Charlemagne. Me, Godfrey (Bloom), Paul Nuttall – both of whom were UKIP MEPs – and Gawain

Towler were proper regulars there. So much so, that if you wanted to get hold of a UKIP quote after office hours during the week, the Kitty O'Shea pub wouldn't be a bad place to start – although leaving it too far into the evening would be a bit of a risk. The Belgian Chimay Bleue dark beer is absolutely delicious, but it is 10 per cent proof.

O'Farrell's – unfortunately a fast food outlet now – was also a favourite, along with the Old Hack pub by the EU Commission. We provided so much business for O'Farrell's that when the British National Party managed to get elected in Brussels in 2009 and adopted the same pub as their local, I had to have a quiet chat with the manager. It was certainly awkward, but the last thing I wanted was to be photographed with one of that lot. Needless to say, it was swiftly dealt with and the BNP were not seen again in there, at least not by me: the landlord simply could not afford to lose our business.

Just before the 2004 European elections, Michael Howard, the ghastly Tory leader at the time, urged Conservatives running as candidates to label UKIP as 'cranks and political gadflies'. He was scared because our anti-EU ticket was playing very well within his own party.

Anyway, in honour of him, I set up the Gadflies Club – a dining club – and we got together every month on the Tuesday that we had to be in Strasbourg. It became an enormous event: we would usually hire a private room in a hotel or restaurant in Strasbourg and invite speeches – usually packed with jokes. It would be an understatement to say that those events are not to everyone's taste. But, for those who did come, it was enormous fun. A lot of people who came along, however, were genuinely appalled.

During that time, it certainly wasn't all drinking. In November 2004, I gave my first big speech in the European Parliament, now that I was the co-chairman of a big Eurosceptic group. It was tremendously exciting.

I had checked, double-checked and triple-checked a background search on the new EU transport commissioner – a Frenchman called Jacques Barrot. He was quite a big cheese. Big because he was the French commissioner and, because of the role, he had quite a sizeable budget. He had just been appointed to the job by José Manuel Barroso and I had found out that he was a convicted embezzler, having funnelled £2 million of government money to his own party's coffers. He was convicted and given a suspended prison sentence. But the French President, Jacques Chirac, had given him amnesty ten years before, which effectively deleted the whole matter. Not for me, however, or the taxpayer.

Barrot never mentioned any of this to the EU Parliament. So, when I stood up and asked why the European Parliament had not been made aware of the new EU Commissioner's criminal background, it was a showstopper. It was quite clear from the expression on Barroso's face that he didn't know about it. Under the French judicial system, a presidential pardon means that not only are you pardoned, but the fact that it ever happened ceases to exist. It is a criminal offence under French law to even say that it had occurred.

Barroso and Barrot were not the only ones to be shocked at the backlash I had unleashed – so was I. I had never come face-to-face with the Continental judicial system before and, I have to say, compared with our own, ours is vastly superior. It also was a big moment for me in exposing how Brussels works as a system and how they stick together.

Sir Graham Watson, the Liberal Democrat MEP, said that in having the audacity to expose an EU Commissioner as a convicted embezzler, I had displayed the worst characteristics of the British football hooligan. That hurt.

The European Parliament President asked me to withdraw my speech so that my words could be expunged from the official parliamentary record or I would face the legal consequences of what I had done. I had no idea that – given that I had made the speech in Strasbourg, therefore in France, not in Belgium – under French law, I could be arrested. I had blithely assumed that I would be protected by parliamentary privilege, but when it came down to it, I just didn't know.

However, it was still a big moment for me. Apart from the fact that I could have been arrested, suddenly I had made a name for myself. I had media requests coming out of my ears. Suddenly, people were listening to UKIP. The footage of my question was disseminated across YouTube in scores of different languages.

There were more positive consequences to come. Relations between Barroso and I remained fantastically frosty for years, and the Barrot outing opened my ten-year battle with the man. The Barrot confrontation really put UKIP on the map in Brussels and it laid the foundations for my next mini coup. I sent written questions to every EU commissioner in early 2005 asking whether any of them had received hospitality or gifts that had not been declared. No reply. I waited. And waited.

Then, in March of that year, at a European Commission meeting, Barroso asked every EU official to leave the room. He addressed the EU commissioners and said: 'I understand that you have got a letter from this Nigel Farage chap. Err. I have a bit of a problem.' He then admitted to the commissioners that he and his family had enjoyed a free holiday on board a yacht owned by the Greek billionaire and shipping magnate Spiros Latsis. At that time, any gift given to an EU commissioner worth more than £103 had to be declared. The holiday – estimated to have been worth about £10,000 – had not been.

What's more, Latsis was one of the biggest recipients of EU money. After the freebie, Latsis received about £7 million in EU state aid. Barroso, of course, said he had done nothing wrong; that he was entitled to go on holiday with friends and family.

Nevertheless, it was very clearly a conflict of interest – and an undeclared one at that.

In the commissioners' meeting, without officials, he then asked round the room whether anyone else had a similar problem. At that, Peter – now Lord – Mandelson's hand went up – surprise, surprise.

He too, he said, may have a problem. He had been on a yacht owned by the co-founder of Microsoft – Paul Allen – for a private New Year party off the Caribbean island of Saint Barthélemy. The software giant had been in a massive legal fight with Brussels, which ended with the EU fining Microsoft £355 million in March 2004 for abuse of its dominant market share.

Needless to say, news of the EU commissioners meeting – and its sordid revelations – leaked. Someone grassed them up. More and more questions were asked. In the end, I tabled a motion of no confidence in the entire commission and started getting signatures from MEPs. Needless to say they hated it, and me.

It led to Roger Helmer, then a Tory MEP, being suspended by the Conservatives for failing to keep in line. Six years later, he would join UKIP. Lots of other people who signed the vote of no confidence were also forced to withdraw their signatures. It was one hell of a game. But I got my day for the vote of no confidence four days before the French referendum, when France was given the opportunity to vote on whether to ratify a treaty on establishing a constitution in Europe. I had the entire commission on a lovely sunny summer's afternoon taking part in the vote – I can tell you, they would much rather have been on holiday in the south of France. Mandelson was extremely sniffy with me. 'Not everything you said about me is true,' he sneered as we went into the vote.

I got up to give my speech – to deliver a motion to sack the entire commission. I talked about the appallingly shabby behaviour of the commissioners.

Roger Helmer stood up and intervened. Didn't I think it was reprehensible that the Tories had forced him to withdraw his signature? Yes, I did, I replied. It was enormous fun causing so much trouble.

Barroso then said that, of course, *I* would never be found on a yacht because I haven't any friends. Pretty puerile stuff.

To have orchestrated such a move – which was high profile on the eve of the French referendum, exposing Barrot, Barroso and Mandelson – was a big moment for me. They were all in hot water. But I felt finally that I had 'arrived' in Brussels.

I went to Paris for the French referendum and stayed overnight, desperate to be there when the results came in. The atmosphere was electric: 55 per cent of French voters who went to the ballot box voted against the ratification, and it left the EU with a huge amount of uncertainty. I was with French politicians partying until dawn. I had done a bit to help the campaign – the Sunday before I had attended a rally of about 7,000 people and told them to '*Dites leurs non*'. My French is not great.

A few days after the French had voted no, was the Dutch referendum. Ahead of it, I organised a get-together in the press bar of the European Parliament, where we had invited 100 or so Eurosceptics. At the referendum, almost 62 per cent voted no. I was euphoric. It felt like we had turned the tide. We were certainly very happy with ourselves and there were huge celebrations: champagne corks popping – the lot.

Outside the press bar was Joe Leinen, a German Socialist who worked very closely with Jacques D'Estaing in drafting the constitution. He was giving press interviews down the corridor and, as I made my way towards him and offered him a glass of champagne, he turned to me and said: 'You may have your little victory but we have fifty other ways to win.' And with that he turned on his heels and walked off.

What followed was disgraceful. They rebranded the project as the Lisbon Treaty, and publicly boasted that, by calling it a treaty and not a constitution, it did not require a referendum to push it through. A few weeks later, the Lisbon Treaty was born – with not a single EU Commission power being given up.

Before the Lisbon Treaty was signed, I had met up with some Eurosceptics from across the political spectrum. I said to them: 'Look, I've done my best but they have cheated.' As far as I was concerned, from that moment it was no more Mr Nice Guy. And many of them agreed with me. The Lisbon Treaty turned me into an enemy of the entire EU project – it wasn't just that I wanted the UK out of the EU, I now wanted the EU brought down. What the Lisbon

Treaty did was cheat us out of the right to vote on the constitution of the EU.

José Sócrates, the Portuguese Prime Minister, tried to speak in the Parliament but several times he had to be stopped because there was so much heckling and barracking from the floor – I was the ring-leader of all of that. It was a bit like being at school.

When the ceremony to sign the Lisbon Treaty came up two years later, I was the last person to speak to David Miliband, then British Foreign Secretary, before he signed it. I said to him: 'Remember you promised us a referendum.'

The Irish were supposed to have held a referendum on the proposed EU constitution the following year. I helped them organise their 'no' campaign. I had had a hunch that we might be able to get our hands on the EU Parliament MEP information budget. The fund had been set up to help pay for the dissemination of information to EU members. I got together with various EU lawyers and they confirmed that, no, there was nothing to stop me and the Irish using that money to campaign against ratifying the constitution.

With that money, we produced an eight-page colour

booklet at a cost of €250,000. All of the Eurosceptic groups chipped in with the amount to which we were entitled, and the Irish Post Office agreed to distribute it. The booklet spelt out why Irish voters should think very carefully before voting to ratify the constitution. It also featured a graphic that really upset Brussels, as I knew it would. The graphic was a syringe, next to which was written: 'Can you be sure that under EU law euthanasia will not be introduced?' That sort of thing certainly upsets people in predominantly Roman Catholic Ireland. The result came in and it was a no.

A few days later I turned up in Strasbourg for one of the most dramatic debates of my career.

Martin Schulz, then chairman of the German Socialists in the European Parliament, declared that Europe must not bow to populism, that the 'no' vote in three EU member states opened the door to fascism. I couldn't believe it. They voted no but a German politician says that their vote should not count – unbelievable. If any last push was needed for me to hate them, it was that.

So, between 2004 and 2006, I became well known as the most controversial member of the European Parliament. I was certainly the most recognised MEP in Brussels, but in Britain, no one batted an eyelid. Nobody noticed what we were doing over there.

The BBC did their best to ignore Brussels and British newspapers would just stick stuff on Brussels in their foreign news pages. What happened in Brussels simply wasn't seen as being relevant to the British public, despite the fact that, increasingly, our own inherited freedoms and rights were signed away to nameless technocrats in Belgium. Despite the fact that most of our laws are drawn up in Brussels, the British media doesn't think that the EU matters. Trade deals, energy policy, employment law – all of it is dictated by Brussels, not Westminster.

I felt increasingly deflated and, by 2007, I really began to wonder whether it was all worthwhile. What was I doing in Strasbourg once a month? During my eight-hour drives there I had plenty of time to think about what I was – or rather, wasn't – achieving as an MEP. I felt that I had gone as far as I could – I simply couldn't reach a wider audience.

Little did I realise that YouTube and social media sites were about to save me. The irony is not lost on me. I never send emails, I stick to texts and I hate technology with a passion, but it would be the internet that would save me in the end.

Throughout 2008 and 2009, the growth of YouTube meant that people in Brussels would post videos of my speeches on the internet that would get tens of thousands of hits around the world. Finally, I was able to reach really big audiences. People in the UK got to know me through YouTube, having been nothing to those who had relied on the mainstream British media to get their news. I began to cheer up.

YouTube was not the only major development to save my career – by 2007, the global financial crisis was brewing, all leading up to the collapse of Lehman Brothers, the Wall Street bank, in October 2008. With my background working in financial markets in the City, I could see only too clearly that London, New York and the big financial centres across Europe were in for it. And I gave speeches on it that were picked up across Wall Street and the City.

What I could see as plain as day was that, what started as a housing crisis – the rise of mortgage defaults – would spread to become a banking crisis, and that in turn would develop into national economic crises. We would then have a nightmare euro crisis on our hands.

I had long predicted that the reason the eurozone monetary union would not work as a project was because member states were not sufficiently compatible. Economic and monetary union could work for Germany and a few surrounding states, but it was plainly obvious that Mediterranean countries and Ireland were too incompatible culturally and economically to be able to fit into one model. It wouldn't work when the markets were doing well and it certainly wouldn't work when they were under stress. It was always going to be Germany that would end up having to try to save the euro project with its proud post-war tradition of a strong and stable deutschmark. But, frankly, the German currency is a million miles away from the Greek drachma. Let's face it: the two countries have vastly different work ethics, to put it delicately. To top it off, not only was the whole European project flawed, Brussels deliberately cooked the books of new, later member states to make sure that they were eligible to join Europe. The European Union was never about monetary union, it was always about political union. And Barroso was the cheerleader in chief.

The effective overnight halving of interest rates and the astonishing amount of EU funds used for massive infrastructure spending in Spain, Portugal and Ireland over a seven-year period created a phenomenal false boom. Over that time, their economies were pumped up with free money. They would never have crashed so far had they never been inflated so much by the Brussels machine.

All excessive parties leave hangovers, and that period of fiscal intoxication was always going to leave lasting damage.

In 2008, I gave a speech in the European Parliament and asked if anyone in the room had noticed the bond spread differential between German and Greek government bonds. No? I was not surprised. None of them had a clue what I was talking about. But, with my background in the City and finance, I kept a very close eye on capital market movements. It might sound technical but what the numbers showed, in all their detail, was how the whole European project was beginning to show enormous strain. Under the mad European model, there was only one interest rate, set by the

European Central Bank, for all countries who had bought into the euro. One size fits all. Except that it doesn't. It does not take a Wall Street whizz-kid to work out that if you buy debt from the German Bundesbank, there is less risk of it defaulting than if you buy it from the Greeks. So it should therefore be priced differently.

When the US Treasury allowed Lehman Brothers to go bust in the autumn of 2008, it triggered a financial crisis that the world had not seen since the 1930s. Massive corporations suddenly saw their order books dry up. Profit warnings from the likes of Intel followed within days. And what was swiftly to follow was the horror that AIG, the insurance giant, needed to be bailed out. Once Wall Street imploded, it did not take long for the crisis to hit Europe. There were then questions over whether Mediterranean governments would be fit to pay their debt obligations. The European debt markets tanked and anyone who knew anything about capital markets wondered whether Spain, Portugal, Italy and Greece were actually about to go bust. Within two years, half of all Spaniards between the ages of eighteen and twenty-five were unemployed. The Greek economy shrank by a quarter, which was a contraction far worse than anything seen in the 1930s. The bailouts followed.

What the financial crisis of 2008 exposed was the catastrophic lack of confidence the global financial community had in the euro. Suddenly, there was enormous interest from the rest of the world in what Brussels was going to do about the crisis: how would the EU backstop the losses haemorrhaging across the eurozone? What, ultimately, the world wanted to know was whether the eurozone could hold itself together and whether the euro could survive. When I gave a speech in the Parliament, it was broadcast on YouTube and I was getting hundreds of thousands of hits.

All the senior players in Brussels were united on one issue. They had all bought into the political vision of an integrated Europe. It didn't matter that they couldn't make the economics work. From Barroso to Schulz, there was only one answer to the euro crisis. It was 'More Europe', more integration. If the European project appeared not to be working, then we needed more of it. More centralised power in Brussels.

Little did I realise when I awoke on Monday 15 September 2008 to the well-trailed news that Lehman Brothers was about to declare itself bust after 158 years of doing business, that it would open massive new opportunities for me.

Courtesy of YouTube, other social media sites and the likes of Zero Hedge, I had a big following in the financial communities of Wall Street and Hong Kong. Not only was I recognised as someone who had worked in the City and understood how global capital markets worked, I was in the thick of it, in Brussels. Wall Street and Hong Kong were desperate to get an insider's view on whether the euro would survive the financial crisis and how far the European machine would go to bail it out. The euro was only six years old as a real, effective currency.

The 2008 financial crisis led to an existential crisis for the entire euro project. It looked like, without bailouts, basket economies such as Greece would have to extricate themselves from the single currency, but no one had a clue how that would work. Every pro-Europe nutter had worked out how to cook the books and get a country into the euro, but no one had worked out what would happen if a country had to leave.

There were some very tense and dramatic debates on the

floor of the European Parliament. Literally from the date of the collapse of Lehman Brothers in September 2008, I received so many invitations to speak at financial conferences across the world I could have done nothing else but attend speaking functions for six months. Investment banks invited me to speak in Hong Kong, New York, London and Zurich.

I seemed to spend much of the next eighteen months on a plane. All any investment banker and economist who hosted me during that period wanted to know was whether the euro and the European project could weather the storm. I told them that no matter how much it defied logic, no matter how much it looked likely that the eurozone should fracture, they must never forget the amount of political capital that had been invested in Brussels, and that the vested interests of the European political class would do everything to keep the eurozone intact.

However, I also told them how bad I thought it was going to get. The financial uncertainty in the US and the downturn inflicting the world's biggest economy would, of course, exacerbate problems in the eurozone. If America had a problem with over-extended mortgages, that was nothing compared with what was about to happen in Spain and Portugal.

My message was that, in the short term, the euro and the eurozone would survive, because there were too many vested interests that would never allow it to fail, but that, in the medium and long term, it would experience a slow and miserable death. Things can always take us by surprise and happen overnight – but I stand by that.

At the conferences, they were also desperate to know whether Brussels would introduce quantitative easing, as London had done to flush the markets with cheap money and keep the system going. I told them that one of the most significant consequences of the global financial crisis was the decoupling of France and Germany – the parents of the European project. Far from converging as two of the most important economies in the EU, they were instead diverging. The political situation in France was far from stable and its economy was sliding. I told anyone who would listen to sell France – French bonds, French shares, the lot.

In 2008, what had been clear was that there was a distinct north/south split in the EU – how stable, robust countries such as Germany were some economic, cultural and political distance from their Mediterranean neighbours. What I had not bargained for was the east/west split that would separate France and Germany.

One real problem with the European Parliament's handling of the financial crisis, and communication of what Brussels was doing to the rest of the world, was the utter paucity of talent among EU politicians, particularly on a senior level. Barroso had absolutely no understanding of capital markets – he just did not have a clue what was happening or what crisis would hit next.

I remember delivering a speech on the floor of the European Parliament in 2010. The mood was very grim indeed. You could see the fear in their faces. I stood up and said to Barroso: 'You look like you've seen a ghost.' For that period, it really was my brand against the world. Barroso had no idea what to say. They really were a talent-free bunch. But they were a talent-free bunch on which I made my name. I had a blast poking fun at them and they had no idea what to do about it.

I think it is fair to say that I managed to ruin the career of

Herman Van Rompuy, who was appointed president of the European Council in 2009. No doubt he felt that as leader of Europe, speaking for 500 million people, it was the pinnacle of his career, having been the Prime Minister of Belgium.

Unfortunately, courtesy of my speech to him and about him in the EU Parliament, if you type his name into the Google search engine, you get me. In the February of 2010, I was mulling over making a speech about him, about the fact that no one had heard of him, and why, as an apparent unknown, was he responsible for leading half a billion EU citizens and earning more than Barack Obama. But I prefer talking unscripted, and I had only got as far as coming up with the line: 'Mr Van Rompuy, who are you? No one has ever heard of you.'

When I stood up to castigate this unknown no-hoper, I had no idea what else I would say. What I came out with effectively wrecked his career and his reputation.

Among other things, I said that we were told that we would get a political leader with the status to lead 500 million people who would represent us on the world stage and be such a name that he would stop traffic in Beijing.

Everyone had assumed that that person would be Tony Blair. Although I suspect being president of Europe would be too lowly for Blair's ambitions – he would want a bigger role.

Instead, I told the Parliament, 'What we got was you!'

'I don't mean to be rude,' I said, 'but you have the appearance of a damp rag and the charisma of a low-grade bank clerk. Sir, you have no legitimacy. We don't know you, we don't want you, and the sooner you're put out to grass the better.'

The European Parliament erupted in a cacophony of protests. How could I be so rude? How could I have insulted the president of Europe in this way?

Unlike the House of Commons, there is only one microphone that feeds to outside broadcasters and it is the microphone of whoever is speaking at the time. So, listening on YouTube or watching it on the television you would have no idea what a racket it triggered.

There was a break in the simultaneous translations that are piped into everyone's ears to accommodate the different languages spoken in the Parliament because, while EU interpreters are among the best linguists in the world, they were stumped to find the translation for 'damp rag'.

The purpose of my speech, no matter how impolite, was not just to be funny. It had a very serious point behind it. Who was this man with one of the most powerful roles in world politics? I work in politics and I had only vaguely heard of him. If I didn't know who this bloke was, what hope had anyone in the UK? Even as a former Prime Minister of Belgium, he still wasn't even on the world's list of leading Belgians.

It became clear to me that Angela Merkel, the German Chancellor, and Nicolas Sarkozy, the then French President, had worked out that if they chose a big fish for the European presidency role it would demean their own leadership on the world stage, so instead chose an unknown who would not upstage them.

I think I was particularly unpleasant to him because I had had to listen to a seventeen-minute dirge from him just before. It was ghastly.

As I sat down, the noise from hecklers, furious that I had the audacity to question the legitimacy of the European president, rose. The general noise was made a lot louder by UKIP MEPs cackling with laughter. I returned to my seat and thought that they hadn't seemed too keen on my speech.

The president of the Parliament – a man called Jerzy Buzek (a perfectly nice chap under normal circumstances) – rose to condemn me and say that this sort of speech must never happen again. It did feel a bit like being at school.

As I left the chamber, the mass ranks of the media were waiting outside for me. I didn't need to do any interviews. After the 'low-grade bank clerk' remark I thought I had said everything I needed to say on the subject. So, I got back to the office and within an hour there was a phone call from an official working for the president of the Parliament. Could I attend a meeting in his office at 9 a.m. the next day?

It was – to coin a City phrase – an interview without coffee. It was me, an aide, Buzek and one of his officials in his very smart office in the European Parliament. The atmosphere was frosty to say the least. I was prepared for a 'books down the trousers' moment.

Buzek, a former Polish Prime Minister, asked me to apologise to the European Parliament. He said that I must apologise to Van Rompuy and, best of all, I had to apologise to the people of Belgium. (I had said in my speech that Belgium was a 'non-country'.) It was at the last demand that I started to fall about laughing. Sorry, Tintin! It was too funny for words.

He pointed out that unless I apologised, he would levy the maximum fine on me. I think they banked on me backing down when faced with the prospect of a financial sanction. They must have thought that I would buckle and apologise because, having left the room after declining his offer to apologise in no uncertain terms, there was a mass of media outside his office, all shouting at me: 'Are you going to apologise?' They had clearly been tipped off about the meeting and its agenda, not least because most journalists don't get up that early in the morning for no reason.

So I faced them and called for silence. 'Ladies and gentlemen,' I said. 'There is a time and a place to admit that you've been over the top; to admit that you have got it wrong and when you have to stand up and apologise. I now apologise unreservedly to bank clerks all around the world for any offence I may have caused them.'

Then I laughed and walked back to the office. The journalists were quite shocked. Most of that lot who work in Brussels have bought the EU project hook, line and sinker and they tend to be very pro-Brussels. To be fair, they have to be – no one would leak them stories if they were Eurosceptics.

Needless to say, I was fined €3,000. But boy, was it worth it.

The Van Rompuy speech went viral across social media platforms. It made the national media. Michael White of *The Guardian*, a true gentleman, wrote a piece about hearing this rancour from the European Parliament from his kitchen radio. Some middle-class types back in the UK thought it was a bit rude, but what we discovered over the next five years was that what we would come to see as a core UKIP voter would just absolutely love it. People laughed – and they laughed a lot. But, as has been the case throughout my political career, I didn't just do it for the laughs. I am not a stand-up comedian. I was making a serious point. These people who run Europe run our lives. They control our governments. Yet they are unelected. Their promotion is sewn up by leaders across the Continent, who have only one thing on their minds – the ever-increasing power of the European project.

Funnily enough, Van Rompuy made himself remarkably scarce after my speech. He was supposed to address the European Parliament after every EU summit, but didn't. He managed to wriggle around appearing in Parliament by instead addressing a committee, so that it was much more low key and I couldn't attack him. Very cowardly. I have seen him maybe five times since the speech and he is very wary. Once, in private, he eyed me very carefully and asked when I was planning to deliver another speech about him. I don't think anyone had ever spoken to him like that before.

There were exceptions to the rule in Brussels. Not everyone was as useless as Van Rompuy.

It was clear after Peter Mandelson was appointed EU Commissioner for Trade in 2004 that he was a highly intelligent political operator. He was impressive. It was also clear to me from his inauguration hearing that he was a master of the brief. It was difficult to trip him up in political arguments. He got into a bit of hot water because of his fondness for billionaire yacht owners, attracting allegations that his influence in Brussels could be bought, but in the context of what he was asked to do as a commissioner, it was clear that he was in charge.

Unfortunately for the EU, when Mandelson had his rapprochement with Gordon Brown back in the UK, it resulted in him leaving Brussels and going back to Westminster to bail out the Labour government. I was not prepared for who Brown would replace him with.

In the past, EU commissioners from Britain were all failed chancellors, former Cabinet ministers or ex-opposition leaders who were heading for obscurity. Suddenly we were lumbered with the noble Baroness Ashton. No one had ever heard of her. She had achieved nothing. Why was she appointed the most senior Briton in Brussels? Not only that, but Brown had given her the Foreign Affairs brief, having given up the all-important trade job that Mandelson had held. It meant that she was the most senior British bureaucrat in Europe. It was quite extraordinary.

I hounded the Baroness in the early days with a repeated

series of questions. I pointed out that she had risen without trace but that the distinguishing feature on her CV was that she had been the treasurer of the CND (Campaign for Nuclear Disarmament) for years under Bruce Kent.

Kent, a former Roman Catholic priest who had been chairman of the CND, had admitted that the movement had taken money from the Kremlin. I kept asking her time and time again during that period whether she had overseen that relationship with the Kremlin, whether she too had taken money from Moscow.

I never got an answer. It struck me that, given she was the supremo of all EU foreign policy, she should answer to the fact that her position on nuclear disarmament meant that she had been on the wrong side of the most significant foreign policy decision since 1945. I felt that this was deeply inappropriate for someone of her seniority in the EU. And I felt it was deeply inappropriate that she refused to even answer questions about her tenure at the CND.

She was a woman who had married well. That was it. No talent, no ability, no skills, no experience. Married to Peter Kellner, the man who runs the polling company YouGov, she had been on the north London dinner party circuit before Blair came to power in 1997. They were New Labour luvvies. When Blair was elected, pretty soon he made her a life peer in the Lords. That was all she had done – and now she was the most senior diplomat in Europe.

Like Van Rompuy, she was utterly useless and when she was placed under scrutiny she just tried to make herself scarce. Occasionally I would see her at the Eurostar terminal in Brussels on the way back to the UK for the weekend. She was always perfectly polite and would wish me a good weekend. I knew she would have a good weekend, given that she never did any work anyway. Mine, I knew, would be flat out.

I hardly saw her in the EU Parliament for months until the issue of whether the EU should intervene in Libya to support the rebels who were trying to overthrow Colonel Gaddafi in the spring of 2011.

Brussels is hopeless at most things, but at foreign policy they are diabolical and dangerous.

Both the EU Parliament and the UN Security Council approved airstrikes on Libya, which began in March of that year.

We had been asked to vote on whether the EU should, with various other NATO states, use our flight power to create a no-fly zone over Libya to protect its people from Gaddafi's onslaught. The cost of maintaining a no-fly zone, where air forces are used to threaten to shoot down any Libyan plane that flies over its own territory, was enormous.

I was against EU intervention in Libya from the start. My Brussels colleagues, to say the least, were not. I found it deeply ironic that the Greens and the Liberals were massively in favour of military intervention in Libya. I suspect they had no real view of Gaddafi and the state of the war, but took this stance because intervention would show that the European Union as a body was able to flex its muscles in a foreign policy and military sense, all of which added to the belief among pro-EU nutters that Europe was getting bigger as a project – that it was no longer just a monetary union but could throw its weight around on foreign policy outside its own borders.

In the same month, I gave a speech on the floor of the European Parliament about EU military intervention in

Libya. In the speech, I said to Baroness Ashton that I was grateful that she was the EU's High Representative of the Union for Foreign Affairs and Security Policy. I was grateful, I said, because if we had someone in that job who was competent and decisive we might actually be quite dangerous. Goodness knows what would happen if we had someone in the job who had a clue what they were doing. She just glowered at me.

UKIP's position on the Arab Spring has always been non-interventionist. I do not believe that there is any appetite of the British people to intervene in yet another Middle Eastern war. I certainly couldn't see how we could make the place better. In the vote in the House of Commons on creating a no-fly zone in Libya, only twelve MPs voted against it. It was extraordinary. Our own national interests were not being threatened and we had no strategy to prepare for what a post-Gaddafi regime would look like. The UKIP position has been proven right. After Gaddafi was killed by his own people, the country has been riven with chaos. One Prime Minister has fled to another country and Libya is now in the grip of Islamist terrorists and has fractured into three parts. It is a country in civil war.

Apart from the political damage we inflicted, just look at the financial cost. I found it deeply ironic that the RAF were flying from north Norfolk in 3,000-mile round trips from Britain to Libya because we no longer have an aircraft carrier.

The war in Syria, which kicked off with pro-democracy uprisings in March 2010, really exposed the complete absence of foreign policy in both Brussels and in London. There was a perceived wisdom that simply wasn't challenged by anyone: it was that President Bashar al-Assad of Syria was the enemy and that the rebel movement fighting his regime were the good guys. Paul Nuttall, my deputy, kept asking in the European Parliament what was known about the rebels. To whom did they pledge allegiance? Who funded them? What did they want, and were they, as Assad had always claimed, linked to terror organisations? William Hague, the then Foreign Secretary, just kept reiterating that we were on the side of the rebels. But, as the war became more drawn out, it proved out doubts were right. One rebel faction – al-Nusra – was closely allied with Al Qaeda and then a new generation of 'rebels' began fighting in northern Syria: the Islamic State, who began kidnapping and beheading Westerners. Suddenly the stability of a regime run by President Assad began to look like the most favourable option. Yet, the complexions of the rebels were never questioned, and many have turned out to be straightforward terrorists.

Whitehall and Brussels had no foreign policy devised for a post-Arab Spring. We had no idea to whom we should try to pledge allegiance and had no intelligence on who was running the region.

By August 2013, Cameron was desperate to show some leadership, and military action in Syria was his ticket.

We were against it from the beginning. Cameron had to go to the Commons and take it to a vote among MPs. On the day of the vote – 30 August – UKIP took out a poster truck and drove it in Parliament Square. It said quite simply: 'UKIP says no to war in Syria'. A few hours later, inside the Commons, Cameron lost and suffered a terrible public bloody nose. MPs voted 285–272 against Britain joining American air strikes on Syria.

What was clear from the polls in the run-up to the Commons vote on Syria was that UKIP had hit a nerve with not only the British public, but also a number of backbenchers who, yet again, found themselves agreeing with our policies.

CHAPTER 6

REFORMING UKIP

IT HAD ALL been going so well. We had hired Central Hall Westminster for the 2013 UKIP annual conference and it was going to be the biggest event we had ever staged.

The venue was terrific – the beautiful Methodist hall with the largest dome in Europe – right opposite Westminster Abbey and a short walk from the Commons. It felt as if we had really grown up, not just because of the grandness of the venue, but because we were launching some good policies and had some great speakers. It was going to be a great day.

At a cost of about £100,000 to host the conference, it was the most expensive event that the party had ever held. What I did not realise on that Friday morning in September was just how much that day would really cost us.

The UKIP conference opened at about 10 a.m. on the morning of 20 September. It was buzzing; plenty of press were there and the lower floor of the hall was already packed out.

Labour and the Lib Dems were having a bad run. That day the *Daily Mail* splashed with the first of its serialisations of the Damian McBride memoirs that revealed the poison and in-fighting at the heart of the Labour Party under Gordon Brown's premiership. Never a bad thing for us.

The Lib Dems had just had their annual party conference and the policy highlight – Clegg's rabbit-in-the-hat moment – seemed to be proposing a 5p tax on plastic bags. A new position on the Asda shopping bag was hardly going to set the world on fire.

So that morning felt good. The conference started with a speech by Roger Helmer, our UKIP MEP and spokesman on energy. He launched the policy that profits from shale gas should be invested in a sovereign wealth fund. Not only is it a good idea, it's a good idea that broadened the UKIP policy menu from issues such as immigration and the EU referendum. It was part of the process of us growing up into a broad, fully formed party, not a single-issue movement.

Mark Littlewood, director of the Institute of Economic Affairs, the free market think tank, was next up. His speech was pretty compelling – good number-crunching on how the coalition had actually reduced government spending by just 1 per cent a year, despite all their bragging and austerity rhetoric. It was good for Kippers to hear it from him, not least because the think tank is non-political, and sweet for me, because Mark used to work for the Lib Dems.

I was up just before noon to give my conference address. Apart from the fact that I regretted writing my speech, instead of delivering it off the cuff – the only time, and the last time I will ever do so – I thought it went well. I predicted that we would win the European elections the following May, and do really well in the local elections on the same day.

After that, I listened to the lunchtime news, and the

line the various news programmes were going with was, 'Shale gas profits should be invested in a sovereign wealth fund' and 'Farage predicts European election win'. All good stuff. This happy state of affairs would last less than two hours. By the middle of the afternoon, Godfrey Bloom, the UKIP MEP whose forthright views had got the party into enormous trouble before, was attending an event to promote the number of women in politics. Godfrey cracked what he said was a joke. Except that it wasn't funny. At the meeting he branded all women in the room sluts, saying they were the type of women who failed to clean behind their refrigerators. Apart from being a bit mad and ill judged, it had three damaging consequences. It reversed the work we had done in trying to make the party relevant to women – convincing them that UKIP is not just for grumpy old Tory men in the Shires. On a bad day, UKIP can look so blokeish – and I am as much to blame for that as anyone else – that we resemble a rugby club on a day out. Second, it played into the hands of those who accused us of being a party of fruitcakes, and third, because for all the effort and money that conference day had taken, the news agenda of the day was dominated by Godfrey. I was furious.

Within minutes of his comments at the event, Twitter started going berserk. There were calls from the media and party members for him to step down. There is no way you can erase that sort of thing, but I at least tried to contain it. I said that Godfrey would have to be disciplined by Steve Crowther, the party chairman. Later on in the afternoon, Godfrey, who was our defence spokesman, gave his speech to the conference. But the only story now was Godfrey's awful remarks. And the problem was about to get a lot worse.

As he left the hall, he was interviewed by Sky News on camera. He just kept digging. It was a joke, he claimed, and the women in the room laughed, he said. When the Sky reporter kept going, he branded him a 'sad little man'. Michael Crick, the Channel 4 journalist, then asked Godfrey why there were no black faces on the cover of our conference guide and Godfrey just exploded. He then hit Crick over the head with the guide, called him a racist and stormed off down the street, threatening an ITV journalist with the same treatment if he didn't show him some respect.

It was just awful and looked ugly. By the evening news, nobody could care less about our new policies, about the progress we were making, about the promise of electoral success the following May; Godfrey dominated everything. All the work we had done had just gone to waste. Godfrey had, in one afternoon, given ammunition to the likes of Cameron, who said in 2006 that UKIP members were all 'fruitcakes, loonies and closet racists'.

I made a statement saying that I thought that the party should withdraw the whip from Godfrey, effectively forcing him to resign. That is exactly was Crowther did. Godfrey was out. And it had been a terrible day.

I have since wondered whether Godfrey had had a drink when he made the remarks. He certainly had a few drinks the night before when he was spotted at the East India Club on St James's Square. But, actually, I think on the day he had only had a couple of glasses of champagne at one of the conference events. So he didn't even have that excuse.

What I could kick myself over is that while Paul Nuttall, the UKIP deputy leader, and I were both very friendly with Godfrey, we both saw the Godfrey car crash coming and failed to act. We had only had dinner with him ten days before, and it was obvious then that he could not control himself. It was only that summer that he had highlighted that Britain spent £1 billion a month on foreign aid – much of it going to 'Bongo Bongo Land', he said, when the country could least afford it. The terrible shame about those remarks is that he had a point, it was just the ghastly and outdated way in which he expressed them.

What Godfrey failed to realise is that what is seen as funny in the officer's mess after a few pints simply looks terrible on public view.

Apart from the fact that he played to all the prejudices that the Tories and Labour promulgate about us, I regret the fact that it abruptly brought to an end what was an enduring twenty-year friendship. Godfrey and I had shared a flat in Brussels, for goodness sake, and we had had fun times. He was one of my closest friends in Brussels and certainly one of my best drinking buddies. We have spoken a little since then with each other, but the relationship only deteriorated further. I regret that. But I also regret what Godfrey did that day.

Firing Godfrey in a way made us look like we were trying

to grow up and clean up the party. But the real, long-term consequence of the incident is that you end up in a situation where politicians are so scared of causing offence that everyone says the same thing, which means they are effectively all saying nothing.

The Godfrey gaffes triggered change within the party. After that I was forced to face up to what I had known for years – that we had to start being much more professional in the way that we chose prospective parliamentary, MEP and local candidates. That there would have to be a system of vetting and discipline that would make sure that we were not exposed to Godfrey moments again.

Vetting new candidates is now handled by David Soutter, who used to work for Conservative central office. Apart from criminal background checks, they are also put through an extensive interview process. Hopefully that makes sure the best candidates get to run. But these problems will never go away completely, and they are problems that are shared by all the parties.

Both us and the Conservatives were burnt by Amjad Bashir, once our communities spokesman and MEP for

Yorkshire & the Humber. We had been investigating him over unanswered financial questions and we had suspicions that he had interfered with the UKIP candidate selection process. Worse, he refused to sever his ties with Mujeeb Bhutto, who had been jailed for running a kidnapping gang in Pakistan. Bhutto had himself been a member of the Conservative Party and then he joined us. He then tried – and was blocked from – re-joining the Tories.

But when Bashir announced that he was leaving UKIP to join the Conservatives in January 2015, the whole thing blew up in both parties' faces.

We had issued a statement saying we were investigating him, and had passed what we believed to be evidence of his wrong-doing to the police just as he was quitting to join the Tories. They clearly had not done any checks on him. They had no idea. Cameron – on learning that Bashir was joining them – issued a gushing statement, saying that he was absolutely delighted. He talked about Bashir's inspiring story of how someone can come to the UK with very little and make something of themselves. The Tories clearly had done no background checks on him at all. It just goes to show how hard it is trying to vet candidates. But I could have kicked myself. Just like Godfrey, I had had bad feelings about Bashir and, only the month before, had wondered whether we should have kicked him out of the party.

*   *   *

I doubt Bashir will be the last to embarrass us and I suspect that we'll still have local council candidates saying things on Facebook that are bad – but so does every party, and nobody notices or cares much.

While quite clearly we do not want people like Bashir, there is a risk of going the other way. If you vet out everyone who is a bit different, who might – perish the thought – express a view they actually believe in, rather than one they think the media and voters want to hear, you end up with the sort of clones that populate the Labour, Tory and Liberal Democrat camps – all of whom went to Oxford to read politics, philosophy and economics, and all of whom look and sound the same. I think it is for the fact that UKIP candidates don't look and sound like the rest of the political class that voters like us.

It is one of the biggest dilemmas of my leadership of the party. What do I want UKIP to look like? Do I want to turn it into a Blairite political party where everyone has a pager, where everyone is 'on message' and no one is allowed to think or speak for themselves? No, I do not. The whole point about why UKIP exists is that we are a party that wants to change things, a party that wants to be radical, and you can't do that without pushing the boundaries of debate. When I said that we should examine the role, structure and funding of public health systems in Europe, it was as if I had said I want to charge every woman of child-bearing age in the UK £19,000 to have a baby. It was extraordinary. The political class simply wants to reinforce the status quo, any fresh thinking – such as how on earth we are going to fund the NHS with a rising and ageing population – is simply rejected out of hand.

A wise general picks his battles, and I don't want candidates who trigger massive distractions, but if you put me up against a wall and ask 'does UKIP become some ghastly politically correct movement or one that lets debate and opinion flow?', I will always pick the latter.

That said, over the years I have grown tired of feeling that for every step forward I took, some exhibitionist looking to make a name for himself would say something that put us two steps behind. I could have done without Dr Julia Gasper, the UKIP branch chair in Oxford, claiming that some homosexuals would rather have sexual intercourse with an animal. I mean, really...? We do have people in UKIP who say silly things, but hardly any of them are uttered by senior members of the party, and very often they are spoken by local councillors.

Every party has these exhibitionists with deeply odd views, but no one notices them – they certainly get no coverage from the media. Indeed, any off-colour remark is almost always confected by the media into Westminster outrage. In the run-up to the European elections in May 2014, UKIP councillors were making front-page news; they were leading news bulletins. Yet at the same time, the arrest of thirteen councillors drawn from Labour, the Conservatives and the Liberal Democrats for a range of offences, from racial violence to child pornography, garnered no coverage in the newspapers at all. Not a word. It is difficult after such experiences to not think that there is a concerted attempt by the political and media establishments to demonise UKIP. It is quite outrageous.

However, our brand of exhibitionists not only get excessive coverage in the British media, they also draw real concern from our donors.

Paul Sykes – a loyal and generous donor to UKIP, and also a close confidant and friend to me – has said on numerous occasions with his flat Yorkshire vowels: 'There's no more room for more exhibitionists, Nigel. We've got one of those,' (looking at me) 'and that's enough. No more drinkers, no more "characters".' Paul, who rarely drinks, said it only partly in jest.

But I feel passionately that if you want to try to coax working-class people back into politics so that the political class stops resembling that fool Miliband, you have to accept that some of them will be a bit rough around the edges. They are going to say things that aren't washed through public relations departments. That's life.

When Emily Thornberry, the former shadow Attorney General, tweeted a picture of a house draped with the flag of St George and a white van parked outside during the November Rochester & Strood by-election, to basically mock the working classes, it just goes to show how entrenched the snobbery against working-class people is in the UK. There is a snobbery across both the media and the British political class about the thoughts and pronouncements of the working classes, and UKIP has certainly coaxed people from very working-class backgrounds into politics.

Jim Carver, the UKIP MEP, is a former market trader from Kent. Paul Nuttall, UKIP MEP for the north-west and our deputy leader, is from a working-class family in Liverpool. He taught history at a further education college. Unlike Cameron, Nuttall's father-in-law was not a millionaire baronet. Britain's political class has long ago dumped the concept of drawing MPs from the communities on whose behalf they are supposed to be acting.

While the Godfrey incident was the worst public bust-up since the Robert Kilroy-Silk debacle in 2004 (when he criticised the then leader of UKIP on television and said that he had ambitions to not just be a UKIP MP, but to lead the party), I am really proud of the people we have now got on board and we have gone some distance to professionalising the party.

Stuart Wheeler had said that he would be UKIP treasurer until the European elections in May 2014, and he has brought real authority and respectability. Unlike the early years of UKIP when there were far fewer impressive people from whom to choose to be treasurer, I identified a man called Andrew Reid who looked very much like he would fit the bill when Stuart decided to step down from the role.

Andrew had contacted me out of the blue in 2011 and invited me to the offices of his law firm. He was one of the founding partners of a law firm called Reid Minty, now RMPI. A litigator, he would make his money out of competition and commercial law, but he really made his name from the defamation case of Lord McAlpine, the – now late – Tory Party treasurer. Both the BBC and, later, the Speaker of the Commons' wife, Sally Bercow, were forced to pay damages after falsely labelling him a paedophile.

I had been interested to meet him one-to-one, to say the

least. He had been a prominent supporter of Boris Johnson and knew people from all walks of life. Alongside his life as a lawyer, he was a tremendously successful businessman, particularly in the property sector, and trained race horses in his spare time. When I went to meet him at his offices in Brooks Mews in the heart of Mayfair, I could hardly have guessed that, one year on, he would offer the same address to us and give UKIP its first London headquarters in that building. That little mews – easily missed – at the back of Claridge's hotel was about to become extremely familiar territory to me.

Andrew was pretty much convinced by UKIP from the start – he needed no persuading. By then Britain was a year into the Cameron-led coalition and, even though Andrew had been a lifelong Tory, he felt that Conservative policies weren't working and that they really weren't getting anything done. He sticks by fairly sound principles that decent ordinary people need to be given opportunities to get on, and that Britain under the Tories really doesn't provide that.

The Brooks Mews meeting was not our first. We had met several times before at a private members' club in central

London, where he attended a number of dinners that I would host for members, potential members and potential donors. It was obvious that he was excited by what UKIP had to offer.

After the Brooks Mews meeting, he committed pretty quickly to wanting to get involved, and since then UKIP has basically taken over his life – as happens to all of us.

It was not just his support and legal expertise we would benefit from, however. I told Andrew that we desperately needed a London headquarters. Over the years, various donors had given us office space in Regent Street and in Soho, but we needed enough area to be able to base our national media and policy teams, and me, in one place. And London is simply too expensive for us to fund that out of party coffers. It is easy to raise money to fund a campaign, but very difficult to raise cash to cover the operating costs of running a party. We had had headquarters in less expensive places such as Birmingham and Newton Abbot in Devon but we really needed to be based in London. I was regularly doing media interviews in London, having dinners with donors and meetings over policy and strategy. We were able to use an office in what used to be Conservative central office, the building from which Thatcher and Norman Tebbit waved on the night of their general election victory in 1987. Now called Europe House, it is the home of the European Parliament information service, so, as an MEP, I am entitled to use office space there. But it would have been entirely inappropriate and politically dangerous to have tried to house the party there. It was also too small. Still, Smith Square was very handy for the Sky and BBC television studios around the corner on Millbank, and less than a five-minute walk from one of my favourite Westminster pubs – the Marquis of Granby – known within UKIP as 'the Mog'. So in 2012, about half a dozen of us moved into Brooks Mews. It was a great feeling. No longer did every conversation have to be conducted on the phone. Finally we had an office where we could work together in one place.

In 2014, Andrew moved us downstairs to even larger offices where we could even house a small call centre for UKIP activists.

The office, while one of the most expensive addresses in London, was far from plush, however. It felt very much like the offices that hedge funds had set themselves up in in the ten years before they broke out of the City and Canary Wharf. In fact, it was something between a hedge fund office and a warehouse, full of UKIP paraphernalia, boxes everywhere and a few glass-fronted offices for private conversations. There's a big boardroom area, which I have never used – not my thing – and my tiny office at the end, which houses a desk, an ashtray, a few chairs and a small bookcase with a couple of books on cricket and angling in it. Apart from a few political cartoon originals of me and UKIP, you would never know that it was my office. I have never used the computer on my desk and spend most of my time on my mobile. The office was also a complete building site – there were workmen there most of the time and when we moved in the windows were still taped up, brand new.

So Andrew, in addition to giving us our own floor in a fantastic central London location, lent us enormous credibility and became treasurer just after the European elections. He was very much a part of making the party a professional outfit.

When I stood again for UKIP leadership in November

2010 to take over from Malcolm (Lord Pearson), I came in on a ticket that I would professionalise the party, that I would bring in new people whom I had hand-picked for key party positions. Without this new breed we would be unelectable, I was sure of that. The new team would work to draw up realistic target seats and hone our political message.

I also had learnt from the Norwich North by-election of July 2009 that we needed to really get our act together as a party.

While we got our best ever result in a parliamentary by-election – with almost 12 per cent of the vote – we still only came fourth. That was the start of my thinking that we had to reform and become a properly professional party. I spoke to Stuart Wheeler at the time and said that for us to be electable we would need to change. We lacked professionalism, money, drive, real ambitions and were broadly perceived as eccentrics having a bit of fun.

The by-election of Norwich North also made me realise that we needed to change our emphasis. In the past, the issue of a referendum on Britain's relationship with Europe had been our ticket. That had to change. I was convinced that we needed to sell the candidate much harder, rather than be so policy-based. I am sure that the way we promoted our candidate Glenn Tingle played a massive role in getting a 12 per cent result, but we needed to be better at it. I also knew that we did not have a chance of being taken seriously by the national media if we did not try to become more professional. The day after Norwich North, the BBC lunchtime news failed to even mention UKIP – even though we had taken an eighth of the vote. I was livid – the electoral graphic they had put together had no reference to us at all.

I also knew that the old UKIP policy of not standing in local council elections was the wrong approach – focusing solely on getting seats in Westminster was not enough.

So, as I prepared to stand as leader again in late 2010, I began to draw up my wish list of key people I wanted in senior posts in the party.

One of that new breed of professionals was Steve Crowther, who would become party chairman. He had organised the 2010 UKIP conference in Torquay and I had been enormously impressed. It was themed pretty well (the speeches and events we were hosting), but, equally important, the conference had a good, smart look to it. As a former public relations and marketing man, Steve clearly had an eye for presentation.

After the Torquay conference, when I announced that I was standing as leader again, I asked him whether he would like me to ruin his life and make him chairman of the party. When people take these roles, they have no idea how full-on they are. Steve was going to have to be a real anchor for the party as chairman, and it is by far the toughest job in UKIP. Every time someone misbehaves and says daft things, they have to discipline them. He would also have to be someone who was not going to be fazed or mess up on high-profile programmes such as *Any Questions*. The days of me being the only person to appear on television to sell the UKIP cause had to be over. If we were to be a grown-up party that was electable, there simply had to be more faces that voters would recognise and trust.

With Andrew and Steve now properly on board, I started to flesh out the size of our core team. Matthew Richardson, still in his early thirties, I appointed party secretary. An Oxford graduate, he was already an accomplished barrister, having written one of the most important books on cyber-crime. But it was his expertise in electoral law that I was most interested in. He became the most important legal officer we had in the party.

By October 2014, I had managed to get a man called Raheem Kassam on board as my main aide. Raheem had been managing editor in London of an online news agency called Breitbart, which had close links to the Tea Party and the Republican movement in the US.

Both Matthew and Raheem would be instrumental in using their US political connections to broker introductions for me in both New York and Washington.

Alex Phillips handled the television side of things. I had first met Alex when she was a young television presenter for ITV Wales. We were both at the Welsh Assembly elections in 2007 and she interviewed me while I was sitting in the back of an open-top pink Cadillac, drinking champagne with the late, great Sir Dai Llewellyn, 4th Baronet of Bwllfa. He stood in the assembly elections for UKIP and was terrific fun. Alex was in the front with a camera as Dai (nicknamed the 'seducer of the valleys' and brother of Roddy, lover of Princess Margaret) and I discussed UKIP's chances in Wales. It must have made an impression on her because I later discovered that she had made a formal approach to the party asking that if a London-based, national media job came up working for us, she would like to have the opportunity to apply. When John Bufton became our first UKIP MEP in Wales, she went to work for him and joined us in London in 2012.

There was still a smattering of the old guard – Gawain Towler, for example, had been with me from early Brussels days. He had worked for the Conservative Party for years but was fired for his role in producing a publication called *The Sprout* – a far more scurrilous version of *Private Eye* but focused on Brussels. He was deeply connected to the online blogging community, but also had a prodigious knowledge of EU law. In 2005, he started working for our group in Brussels, helped us with the European elections and then just stayed. He is a good asset when some idiot from Westminster stands up and declares that they will do such-and-such in Brussels and he is able to say – quickly and with authority – why what they're saying is a nonsense.

Slowly, with the new team and by expunging the disasters of the old party, we began to look like a proper political organisation. Out with the likes of David Campbell Bannerman, who wrote our unreadable 486-page manifesto, and in with Tim Aker, a young UKIP MEP whom I made head of strategy.

With the hiring of Patrick O'Flynn, a veteran *Express* journalist, and Paul Lambert, the BBC political reporter, I felt we had a strong team. We had had such a rough ride with the British media that taking on two experienced heavyweights was a real coup for us. Patrick knew the political newspaper scene in the lobby like the back of his hand, and Paul – known in the BBC as 'Gobby' – was a veteran within political broadcasting. What they also had in common was that they are both driven and tremendous fun. They have the UKIP brand all over them. Paul's irreverence for the political class, for example, is pure UKIP. He earned the nickname Gobby because he was well known at the BBC for shouting questions at politicians as they went in and out of Downing Street. 'Are you going to resign?' was a common one.

One appointment I would rather not have had to make

was that of James Woolfenden, former British Army man who had been in Afghanistan with the military police. After I was surrounded by around fifty very, very angry Scottish nationalists on Edinburgh's Royal Mile, and then barricaded in a pub, I realised that I was going to need proper security. I felt threatened.

However inconvenient, it was just another part of becoming a mainstream party. I hated the idea of having personal security – part of my political appeal is that I am an ordinary person who you can approach in the street and have a banter with. It went against the grain that somehow there might be a barrier between me and a voter. However, the Edinburgh incident (exposing the very ugly face of Scottish nationalism), and various issues since, have made it unavoidable. Given that as UKIP leader I do not qualify for taxpayer-funded security, the party pays for our own. As an MEP, I seemed to spend my time almost entirely on the Eurostar or driving the eight-hour journey to Strasbourg; now it seems that I am always in the back of the Land Rover accompanied by James and his team. They are great blokes, but I wish I didn't need them.

The following year, I tried to really put in place different ways of campaigning. In the old days, UKIP members would have sought to raise the profile of the party by penning a letter to *The Times*. But I was determined to make UKIP move on. In March 2011, we contested the Barnsley Central by-election, and our candidate was Jane Collins, who was brought up in Yorkshire. As we had done in Norwich North, we made the campaign about the candidate; we made it personal, and it made the campaign look more focused and more relevant to the voter. In national politics, the vote is really about the leader of the party, but in by-elections it is more often than not about the local candidate. Whereas before, with old UKIP, our main campaigning message would have been how Britain must change its relationship with Brussels, this time round we still pushed the EU card, but Jane also pressed local issues. Why, for example, were there six people on Barnsley Council earning more than £100,000 a year each? The strategy began to pay off. She came second to Labour, but, like Norwich North, we got 12 per cent of the vote. Gone were the days of just managing to keep our deposit.

The local elections of 2013 were to be another test of us as a professional party. I was determined to make sure that we fielded a record number of candidates. In the event, we had 1,800 all over the country. For us, this was mega.

In line with trying to keep our political message focused and local, I decided to do a two-week tour up and down the country – I christened it the 'Common Sense Tour'. Starting on 2 April, just over a month before the elections, MEP Ray Finch and I hired an old London black cab and began to tour the UK. It was to be the first outing of the thick yellow corduroy trousers and tweed coat. And it became something of a brand.

We started in Cornwall. It was the coldest of Aprils and there was no heater in the cab. Ray, who had been a security guard for most of his working life, is a Scouser and an appalling driver. At a previous meeting years earlier in Cornwall, three people turned up. It was not a good sign. But we gathered momentum. As we kept going, the crowds got bigger and this time, in the same hall, there were 300 or so crammed in, turning up to listen to what I had to say on Brussels, immigration and the strain it placed on local services. I really worked hard to hone the UKIP message – how Brussels' control and profligacy stymied the ability of local businessmen to run their businesses as they see fit. How uncontrolled immigration made it a nightmare to run a local primary school because head teachers – and the local council – simply had no idea how many new foreign families would be turning up in their area.

I talked about wind farms – in 2013 alone, there were 400 anti-windfarm groups across the country, yet no one in Westminster notices.

When we stopped in the Forest of Dean, we hired the back room of a pub and it was so packed it was like the black hole of Calcutta. My Common Sense Tour took people by surprise – that someone had bothered to leave London and come and speak to them. At the end of my speech in the Forest of Dean pub, a man got up and joked: 'Nigel, you are the Messiah!' To which, I replied, courtesy of Monty Python: 'No, I'm just a very naughty boy.' Another man I met at a pub debate, right in the middle of the two-week tour, remarked about the grass-root response to UKIP: 'Nigel, I don't know whether it's a bang or an explosion, but something is happening out there.'

I think it was the happiest two weeks of my life. The reform plan appeared to be working, we were getting a huge amount of coverage in the local media – they seemed fascinated by UKIP. Alongside being out on the stump most of the day and holding public meetings, I did masses of local media interviews. I really felt that we were getting through to people in a way that we just had never been able to before.

It was exhausting. Mind you, going straight to the boozer every evening followed by a visit to whichever curry house was open the latest and rolling into bed far too late probably didn't help. But I can't think of a time when I enjoyed myself more.

There was another treat in store, however. Back at home, the Sunday before election day, I was watching Sky on the television in my kitchen when Ken Clarke appeared wearing an extraordinary turtleneck pullover, looking like he'd been pulled through a hedge after a very heavy Saturday night. In the interview – asked about the upcoming local elections and the threat of UKIP – he declared that we were a bunch of clowns. Thank you, God! That's another 2 per cent on the UKIP vote. If there is one thing a Tory voter hates, it's being told that if they dare to agree with something UKIP is saying, they are foolish, derisory and racist. I was delighted. *Private Eye*, very bravely, put me on their front page with the headline 'Send in the Clowns'. And they did so even before the results had come out.

Eventually, 2 May came around: election day. I knew it would be a great test to see if, in local elections, we could keep the momentum and grab a decent proportion of the vote. Were we finally about to become a proper, electable, grown-up national party?

I booked into the City Inn hotel in Westminster and watched with both excitement and disbelief as the results were coming in well into the early hours of the next morning. We came third, with about 23 per cent of the vote. The Tories got the lowest percentage of the vote since 1982 and the Liberal Democrats were just walking wounded. I was euphoric.

I was due to be on the BBC *Today* programme on the top slot at 8.10 a.m. for an interview with John Humphrys that morning so I got a black cab from the hotel and made my way to Broadcasting House. The perception was very much that the Conservatives had just not appealed to their core voters. What Tory in their right mind would expect their Prime Minister to spend his time obsessing about gay marriage and support open-door immigration? Cameron just didn't have a clue what Tory voters really thought about anything.

After the interview, I was due to meet Alex and Gawain at the Millbank studios in Westminster at 9 a.m. It was a bright May day, so I decided to walk it, going down Regent Street and St James's, then cutting through St James's Park – one of the most beautiful in London. It gave me time to really think on the year so far and what we had achieved. I had a few smokes on the way, office workers on the street congratulated me and the flowers were out. I was terribly happy. As I turned into Great Peter Street in Westminster, just before the Millbank studios, there was a massive scrum of photographers and cameramen. My first reaction was: 'Blimey. Something big must have happened. I wonder what it is.' It turned out they were waiting for me. I was stunned. Even during my short euphoric walk, I still hadn't quite got it. I still had not managed to grasp just how far we had come and how the results had propelled us.

I went into the studios and did a number of the big news networks – ABC, Sky and the like. By the time I came out of the studios, it was about 10.50 a.m., and there were even more photographers there than when I went in. I literally could not put one foot in front of the other. I knew what they were after.

'Look,' I said, trying to reason with them. 'I know you want a picture of me standing outside a pub, beaming with a pint in my hand. If we go round the corner to the Marquis of Granby on Smith Square and order a pint, will you then leave me alone?'

After that I knew we were on the right track. I knew we were on our way. My life had changed for good.

CHAPTER 7

THE MEDIA, MURDOCH, THE AMERICANS AND THE TEA PARTY

'THE BIG BOSS wants to see you,' Neil Cavuto, the TV anchor of Fox Business News, said to me after we had both come off air.

'Really? Who's the boss of the Cavuto show?' I replied, naively.

'No. Not a producer. The big boss. Rupert,' Cavuto smiled.

I had met Rupert Murdoch once before, at a private dinner at his house off St James's in London. We drank red wine from some vineyard he owned. But that was in March 2013 and he had wanted to talk to me to find out about UKIP and my views on the whole Brussels machine, that sort of thing. But in the eighteen months that had passed since, we had won the European elections and made political history, we were a proper credible force, and Douglas had quit the Tories and joined us. We had plenty to talk about.

A producer took me and Raheem from the studios of Fox News – in the basement of the News Corporation building on Sixth Avenue in midtown Manhattan – up to the seventeenth floor.

Raheem was tickled pink when we reached Murdoch's office. Then I went into his office on my own. We were there about forty minutes or so. Murdoch was as I remembered him from our previous meeting: very, very switched on, with a massive interest in global affairs. He's an important figure for me – he did an enormous amount to persuade Tony Blair to promise to have a referendum before joining the euro. On that, Murdoch basically saved Britain's bacon. I want very much to go back and see him – I am in a very good position to brief him on politics in Europe, especially if we manage to force a referendum on getting out altogether.

On a personal level, we share a lot of common ground. We are both outsiders who despise the establishment, and neither of us has been scared about taking it on. We are both fighters with a mutual contempt for the inherited, innate sense of entitlement of the British political class. And we are both used to being figures of absolute contempt, as well as being subject to the appalling snobbery of the establishment.

My meeting with Murdoch was part of a scheduled four-day trip to the US in September 2014. It was extraordinary in many ways – and not just because of my latest meeting with Murdoch.

Raheem, Matthew Richardson and I had a manic set of meetings planned in New York and Washington, with a view to learn from the Americans how to campaign more effectively, to make new allies on both sides of the political divide and to do some media interviews.

In terms of how to campaign, the Americans are streets ahead of the British.

The Newark by-election on 5 June of that year taught me a painful but valuable lesson. UKIP was far too amateurish about structuring and running a successful electoral campaign. And we needed to learn fast about how to change our ways. By then I knew that we would certainly have two by-elections to fight in the short term (Clacton and Heywood & Middleton) and probably another (Rochester & Strood) in the late autumn. The truth was that UKIP, with far fewer resources that the Labour Party and the Tories, had to be much cannier at learning about the constituents in key target seats. The by-election in Newark had been triggered when Patrick Mercer, the Conservative MP, stood down after he was exposed for not declaring lobbying money. The Tories held the seat, but lost about 9 per cent of their majority. We, on the other hand, came second with about 26 per cent. Had we been more organised and clever, we could have done much better.

So, after Newark, I tasked Raheem with planning a US trip to help us meet campaign experts who worked for both the Democrats and the Republicans. He had good contacts across the pond on account of his previous employment at Breitbart.

We needed to find out how to get information about voting habits, and keep that data up to date so that, on polling day, we could go from one house to the next and know who were swing voters, who would never vote UKIP and who might need to be chivvied up to get out and vote.

In the US, electoral battles are fought so fiercely that both the Republicans and Democrats have become experts at what is known as 'micro-campaigning'. This entails understanding how to use technology to know your voter, basically, to make shortcuts in campaigning. By the time of our September trip, I knew that we had no time to spare to get this kind of expertise – the Rochester & Strood by-election was just over two months away, and we had no real base there. It had been 271st on our target list of constituencies, and we were basically starting from scratch.

Matthew Richardson had spent two years developing contacts in Washington for us, brokering introductions in Washington and New York with Republicans, Democrats, Tea Party types and the media, building a proper profile with the online media community who were critical.

Both the Republicans and the Democrats spent a fortune developing what they call 'micro-targeting'. The system involves garnering as much information about the voters you are targeting as you can onto a database and then deploying what would be our 'People's Army' to canvas them, door to door, slavishly, right up to and including polling day. They call it 'Big Data' in the States. What it means in practice is that by the time you knock on the door of someone in a constituency you are trying to win, you know everything you need to know about their voting habits. The Americans – on both sides of the political divide – were also much better than us at the getting voters out to polling stations. Never more was this the case than the Obama win in 2008. The Democrats had done such a brilliant job at getting turn-out up, eliciting votes from people who traditionally had felt so disenfranchised and disillusioned by the political establishment they would never have bothered going to a polling station. In 2008, there were black Democrat voters who had never voted in their lives before. We needed to learn how to coax our so-called disenfranchised voters out. And we needed to get them to the polling stations in Rochester.

That trip to America also convinced Raheem and I of the extraordinary power of online media and how it had made me and UKIP a massive, albeit surprising, brand in the US.

We simply would not have got the coverage from traditional media. British newspapers long ago gave up covering Brussels properly. There are a few grown-up journalists – and by a few, I mean fewer than five – who have a good understanding of how Brussels works, but their London editors have no appetite in reading about Brussels. So, it was through YouTube and websites that followed me that I began to build a profile, particularly in the States. Frankly, if it had not been for YouTube, I would have given up politics years ago, because I just couldn't get anyone to listen. I do realise, by the way, the extraordinary irony of that statement – my family, friends and close colleagues find it enormously amusing that I am scared of technology. All email traffic goes to my wife – I have no email account – and I despise those hand-held machines waitresses pass you in restaurants to pay the bill. But, that said, I did realise long ago the enormous value of social media networks and the online media community. Even as far back as 2007, I was making speeches on the floor of the European Parliament about the financial crisis, about severe problems for the euro, and challenging the authority of Van Rompuy and Barroso and, before I had even left the Parliament building, they were already on YouTube or being reported on Zero Hedge, watched 4,000 miles away in New York. The speech I gave in 2010 criticising Van Rompuy, when I questioned – in quite colourful terms – his qualifications to lead the 500 million people across the EU, has had millions of hits.

Nowhere was the power of that internet presence more acute than in America. It was extraordinary. Raheem and I were going back to our hotel in New York – the Standard High Line near the Meatpacking District – and a cocaine dealer on the corner came up to me and starting asking me about UKIP. We were speechless, and just fell about laughing. He had seen me on Fox News at some point and had started following me on YouTube. You couldn't make it up.

That following – and the brand it afforded us – really opened doors for me in the US, with the media but, critically, with the political class there. I am always bombarded with interview requests when I am in the States, so much so that I could fill up my whole time there just doing the media. The interest from Fox News is obvious – I am a right-winger who is taking on the political establishment – but requests came from a broad church of media outlets.

Breitbart, for whom Raheem used to work, offered to host a dinner for us on that trip in Washington. They own a large house overlooking Capitol Hill – they call it 'The Embassy' – right next to the Supreme Court.

Breitbart is a smart media outfit, as is Steve Bannon, the former Goldman Sachs banker who runs it. He is certainly my sort of chap. He was in the US Navy and then advised the Pentagon on naval matters under Reagan. After that he joined Goldman Sachs where he worked on M&A. He then set up and ran his own investment firm. Even before I discovered his views on Wall Street and big government, we had plenty in common. I certainly didn't know him when I was in the City, but I began to follow him when he made the documentary *Generation Zero* in 2010, about the role of the Washington political class in the financial crisis two years before. It was pretty gripping stuff, and we were definitely singing from the same hymn sheet. In it, he exposed the astonishing incestuousness between Wall Street and Capitol Hill, which manifested itself through the funding of the established political class by big banks, private equity and hedge funds, and how, in return, Washington bailed them out during the 2008 financial crisis. He made another documentary a few years later on the renaissance of conservative American women who were fed up with Obama's worldview that everything should be controlled and provided by central government. He also has some pretty strident views on Obama's insistence that the only way to reform the American immigration system is to grant amnesty to every Tom, Dick and Harry who enters the country illegally.

It was at that dinner that the level of interest in UKIP from the American right really hit me. The evening was massively oversubscribed and there must have been about a hundred people there, from senators to talk show hosts. It was crammed and boiling. I had Laura Ingraham on my left – the conservative political commentator and Fox television news host – and Jeff Sessions, the Republican senator, on my right. Jeff, who is senator for Alabama and a former attorney, is one of the only voices on American immigration now.

I gave a speech on the rise of UKIP, pointing out that two-party politics is not always there to stay, that sort of thing, and then sat down. Pretty much all of them then bombarded me with questions. How do you get attention being a protest party? How do you turn a protest party into a mainstream one? How can you compete with the money and infrastructure of the political establishment? How can you turn really toxic topics – such as immigration – into a mainstream political discussion?

Sitting in this house on Capitol Hill, in the shadows of the political establishment that has embedded itself for centuries, the senators and journalists around the tables showed their appetite for change too, but they didn't appear to know what to do about it.

In the US, of course, they are stuck with two-party politics. Even the Tea Party is a party within the Republican Party. So they were fascinated at the idea of a relatively new party not just existing, but flourishing in the UK. The dinner was after the Newark by-election but before Rochester. They found the UKIP story exciting. In the US, if you look at the history of their various libertarian parties, they never got more than 1 per cent of the vote. We're not libertarians, but they were excited by the fact that a few months before we had won 27 per cent of the vote in the European elections and beaten both the Tories and Labour. They wanted to know how we had done it and, critically, how we had picked really thorny subjects, such as immigration, and made them mainstream issues that all the parties had to address. Immigration is a major issue now in the US, so our stance on limiting immigration in the UK and forcing the Tories and Labour to also come up with a take on border control was very interesting to them.

The September visit would also afford me the opportunity to meet Rand Paul, the Republican senator for Kentucky, and, at the time of writing this book, a frontrunner for the 2016 presidential election and one of the Tea Party's most convincing candidates. Matthew had set up a meeting for the two of us. In an office five minutes' walk from Union Station in Washington, we began to talk about immigration, non-intervention in Syria, and Brussels. Over the course of that half-hour, I realised that in Rand Paul I had found my political doppelgänger. Raheem made the point that you couldn't get a cigarette paper between the two of us on the issues we discussed.

I liked him enormously: he is a realist, he is down to earth and very modest. He certainly comes from a political family – I knew his father Ron – but he is not a career politician. He trained as an ophthalmologist and set up his own clinic, so he knows something of the world. It is unsurprising that UKIP and the Tea Party have plenty in common. The Tea Party has its own share of oddballs and mavericks who sometimes espouse pretty extreme stuff, but they also have truly impressive politicians, like Rand, who believe that the state is too big, too costly, too powerful, and robs the individual of inherited rights and freedoms. They believe that there is no reason why America has to be run like Europe. They came to their conclusions via similar routes as me. The Tea Party did the numbers and took the view that there is simply no reason why the American state should cost more than 30 per cent of GDP (gross domestic product).

I left the meeting thinking that Rand was a man I could do business with in the future – there are plenty within the Tea Party with whom I could not. The truth is their party has been hijacked by the religious right;

if you look at people such as Sarah Palin, they are just downright scary.

Our meetings in New York and Washington taught me a great deal, not least how relationships between the Republican Party and the Tories had broken down. One reason Republican senators were so keen to see me was that they said that the Conservatives didn't bother with them any more. Cameron really is a fool. We need strong relationships across the Atlantic, not least because we learn so much from each other.

One thing, however, that I knew I would not be taking back from the US to Britain was the practice of negative campaigning as espoused by the likes of David Axelrod, President Obama's former chief election campaign adviser, who now works for Ed Miliband. The American practice of 'slagging off', undermining, bullying and trying to dig up dirt on political opponents simply does not sit well with the British electorate. I think voters in the UK are massively turned off by that sort of campaigning; they want a clean fight, to know what you stand for, and for their politicians to show a bit of dignity. Both Mark Reckless and I know at significant personal cost what it is like to be on the receiving end of that sort of negative campaigning – it was frankly shocking to see how the Tories tried to put the frighteners on Mark after he quit the Conservatives and the kind of slurs they made about him were just horrible. I also saw from the television debates that I did with Nick Clegg in the run-up to the European elections that the British public is turned off by aggression, by nastiness. It is fair enough to poke fun at an opponent in a light-hearted way, but it plays very badly when politicians go for the jugular.

The other thing that I certainly do not want to learn from the Americans is their puritanism about booze. I have been travelling to the States for the best part of twenty years and their attitude towards drinking has changed very little, and neither has mine. When I worked in the City, there were some clients who liked a typical Farage lunch – known as the '12 till 12'. I would get in at the crack of dawn and work flat-out until lunchtime and lunch would just, well, carry on. That culture never caught on on Wall Street, and the American puritanism that came with the invasion of the

US banks in the City took a lot of the fun out of London finance. On this trip, I confronted it all over again.

Steve Bannon had scheduled back-to-back meetings for a whole morning. It was non-stop and we just kept going. Senators, journalists, lobbyists – Steve had lined them all up. Finally, at about one o'clock, Steve suggested we break for lunch – a comment that really perked us up. Until Steve followed the suggestion with the horrific phrase: 'I've ordered some sandwiches.' Raheem looked aghast. My feelings fell somewhere between panic and indignation. 'I know I'm the guest here, Steve,' I said, 'but I think it is about time we stopped for a proper lunch.' I refused to budge on it. Americans just don't buy the idea that the working day can easily be done and dusted by 2 p.m. Steve just rolled his eyes and handed me his AmEx card, which prompted me, Raheem and Matt to joyously trot down to a New York steak house, tails up, and immediately get the wine list. Matt had a 27oz burger with a stack of onion rings – halfway through, he began to sweat profusely. It was a corker lunch. We had such a good time I tried to persuade the boys to reschedule our flight home that evening and just get tucked into another bottle of red or two. Had it not been for the small issue of the Rochester by-election, we would still have been there.

CHAPTER 8

SOUTH THANET: MY BID FOR A SEAT IN WESTMINSTER

THE BATTLE TO win South Thanet in the May general election may well prove to be my biggest yet.

If, as Matthew Goodwin, the Nottingham University politics professor and expert on UKIP, predicts, we get between four and six Westminster seats in May, there is a real risk that I may not have one of them.

The risk is that I will have got UKIP to be an electable party; made British political history by beating both the

Conservatives and Labour in a national election for the first time since 1906; and steered the party to get its first seats in Westminster – but also be the only party leader to not have a seat there himself.

My campaign to win South Thanet was supposed to start in September. I had planned a six-month run-up to the general election, slowly building the Farage and the UKIP brands in this small coastal corner of Kent.

But when Douglas Carswell and Mark Reckless both left the Conservative Party to join UKIP in late summer and early autumn, all of the UKIP machine – and my time – was focused on making sure they won the two by-elections they triggered. By the time Mark was safely elected back in Rochester & Strood, this time as a UKIP MP, it was almost Christmas.

So it was not until the cold, dark and alcohol-free days of early January that I was able to properly concentrate on trying to campaign and win a seat for myself in South Thanet.

I assigned Chris Bruni-Lowe, who had masterminded – and won – both the Clacton and Rochester by-elections to run my South Thanet campaign. But, as we discovered from trips I made there in early January, few voters in the constituency even knew I was running as an MP there. I realised then it was going to be a struggle to win.

The consequences of me failing to secure a seat for myself in the Commons would be significant for both myself and the party. It is frankly just not credible for me to continue to lead the party without a Westminster seat. What credibility would UKIP have in the Commons if others had to enunciate party policy in Parliament and the party leader was only allowed in as a guest? Was I supposed to brief UKIP policy from the Westminster Arms? No – if I fail to win South Thanet, it is curtains for me. I will have to step down.

Yes, I love a challenge. I love a gamble. I am at my best when my back is against the wall and the odds are stacked against me. But I could really have done without this particular challenge.

Miliband and Cameron simply do not have to worry about keeping their Doncaster and Whitney safe seats. There is virtually no chance that they will lose and they have constituency teams that run them, giving them the time to lead their own parties and to run their own national election campaigns.

I, however, do not have that luxury. Alongside leading the party, masterminding the general election campaign and leading a group in the EU Parliament, I have to win a Westminster seat from scratch.

Still, choosing South Thanet was not difficult. It was always going to be this constituency. I have represented Thanet since 1999 as an MEP because it falls within my south-east of England constituency.

I stood for the same constituency in 2005, having been persuaded to stand by a local businessman called Martyn Heale. He had real get-up-and-go and knew the constituency well because his business was going door to door selling electricity, persuading people to switch power suppliers, that sort of thing. But he had a political past that kept being dragged up, having once been a member of the National Front in the 1970s though followed by twenty years of Conservative Party membership, so he persuaded me to stand instead of him.

Back then, we got just over 2,000 votes, or about 5 per cent. In those days, that was a pretty respectable result for UKIP – at least we kept our deposit.

This time around, the stakes are high. In the past, it had been a duty to stand there – it was my backyard – even though I knew we had no prospect of winning.

Ever since 2005, I have built a very close relationship with the UKIP local branch and I know the activists there tremendously well. Alan Bown, a Kent businessman who is one of UKIP's longest-term supporters and the second biggest donor to the party, gave us use of a shop in South Thanet for us to have as a constituency office.

Thanet South, as it used to be called, has been a swing seat for decades, having been held by both the Tories and Labour in the last twenty years. It used to be the constituency of Jonathan Aitken, who at times has been a UKIP supporter. From 1997 right up until 2010 it was Labour-held, then it swung back.

In 2010, I didn't stand again in Thanet because I stayed away to fight John Bercow, the Speaker of the Commons, in Buckinghamshire. To be honest, that was just an excuse.

I needed a reason to step down from being leader of UKIP – I was wholly tired of it.

This time around, everything is different. Not only do I have to win it to secure my own political future as leader of the party, but also, on 7 May, along with the general election, the whole of Thanet District Council is up for grabs.

Voters are not stupid. The people of South Thanet know that if they elect a party leader as their local MP, they will not get the same amount of attention that a lower-key politician, with a less onerous workload, would be able to offer them. In short, I cannot win this seat on my own. But I think I can win it if I can show that I am part of a big, strong, active local team to support them, that is enthusiastic and capable. I think that is quite a compelling offer. We will do our best to get enough council seats to control the district council.

The current local MP – a Tory called Laura Sandys – is standing down, citing family pressures. She's a popular local MP, a massive Europhile, and really ought to be a member of the Green Party. But she certainly comes from good

Conservative stock – her father was Duncan, the former Defence Secretary who for a time was married to Winston Churchill's daughter.

Now the Tories are putting up a man who used to be a member of UKIP (and who, bizarrely, was the accountant who wound up my City business Farage Futures – small world) and Labour, a 25-year-old county councillor.

I'm not sure what Conservative voters in Thanet will make of the Tory candidate Craig Mackinlay. The Tories in Thanet are mainly elderly. Equally, solid Labour voters there are traditional Old Labour, yet they have put up Will Scobie as their candidate. Apart from being only in his twenties, he sounds like a Blairite. I'm not sure how that will go down.

Anyway, my campaign strategy for Thanet will be based on how we won Rochester & Strood, but more forensic. On 18 January, we bussed in about 500 UKIP activists and canvassed the whole constituency – street by street, house by house. On that day, we garnered basic, but crucial, voter data. Who were hard-line Tories? Which households were possible UKIP voters? Which ones were solid UKIP and where were the Labour supporters? Equally important, however, was information about what issues they were most worried about. Was it immigration, the NHS or the local airport?

Chris Bruni-Lowe – who masterminded the Rochester by-election – then had a canvas to work from, using our voter database. From there, he was able to leaflet the constituents on specific issues, challenging the Tory and Labour position on them. I am told that I am a divisive figure – a 'Marmite' man – people either love me or loathe me. Chris really made that characteristic work in our local electoral strategy: UKIP campaigners discover very quickly when they are door-stepping which ones despise me. The trick is to give them a wide berth, don't waste time trying to convert them and make sure that on polling day you leave them alone – history has shown that, if prodded, they are more likely to try to block UKIP if they have not already voted.

Critical to the overall plan, however, were public meetings in the constituency. Slicing the constituencies into wards, we sent leaflets to every home inviting them to attend a public meeting close to where they lived to meet me and the team. It would be a chance for them to ask me questions about policies and my commitment to them and to see how impressive the UKIP team were. They were not open to the press and, most importantly, anyone wanting to come had to send off the tear-off strip at the bottom of the letter to book or apply online. That also gave us their email details. We asked those Thanet residents who had already decided to vote UKIP, however, not to come to the meetings. We wanted, we explained, to work on the so-called 'undecideds', not people who had already made up their minds. The meetings were a genuine opportunity to grill me and to debate policy – national, international and local. Chris set the meetings up very forensically – importantly, you could only attend if you lived in the relevant ward.

The meetings were packed out. I was scheduled to do seventeen of them in thirty-five days from January and we were getting around 150 people attending each. We knew they were local because most of them arrived at the venue on foot.

In one, on 21 January, the Ramsgate Round Table hosted a debate in Broadstairs. I was up against the Tory candidate Craig Mackinlay and the Liberal Democrat Russ Timpson. As we arrived, they conducted a quick approval rating poll. On the way in, Mackinlay was on 49 per cent and I was on 15 per cent. On the way out, at the end of the debate, they conducted another poll. This time Mackinlay was at 33 per cent and I was on 36 per cent. That's the kind of swing I need on 7 May.

One of the key decisions we have made in the campaign (nationwide, not just in Thanet) is to avoid negative campaigning. As I'd already seen, it may work wonders in America to trash your political opponents and to try to dig up dirt on them, but it doesn't play well with the British voter. Most people think it looks undignified and it alienates them. I believe in the old saying: 'If you pick a fight with the chimney sweep, you get covered in soot.' No, stick to expressing the positives about UKIP; don't throw abuse at rival candidates and, if they do so to you, rise above it.

While we are trying to keep well away from negative campaigning, the flak against me is quite substantial and I suspect it will only get worse the closer we get to the election. The other parties are obsessed with me not winning a Westminster seat and I can only hope that the hits on me will take the heat off the other UKIP target seats.

Chris and I learnt another very valuable lesson from the Rochester & Strood by-election. Despite the astonishing resources the Tories had deployed on Rochester – they sent forty-five busloads of activists on polling day to get the Conservative vote out – they were selling themselves on national policies, when it was keeping our campaign focused on local issues that helped swing it for us.

So, apart from debating issues such as future NHS funding and immigration, we had a strong local menu. Under the slogan 'A powerful national voice for Thanet', without promising anything, I told voters that maybe, because of my profile and my financial background, I might be able to secure some private investment in the area. Hand on heart, with my background and my contacts, I think I have a better chance of doing that than the other candidates.

Separately, the local council candidates campaigned under the slogan: 'Because Thanet matters'. The issues they raised were properly local ones – street cleaning and excessive parking charges. They also talked at length about Thanet's local airport – Manston – which was bought for £1 by a consortium that included the millionaire Stagecoach boss Ann Gloag. They shut it a few months later with the loss of about 150 jobs. It wasn't just the lost employment: the airport is part of Kent's heritage. That airport was used by the RAF in the First and Second World Wars, by the American military during the Cold War and British Airways tested the Airbus A380 there, as well as the Boeing Dreamliner.

Apart from the fact that a valuable piece of local infrastructure had just been discarded, it also brought it home to constituents, in case they needed any reminder, that Westminster couldn't have cared less about Thanet. There was no interest from Whitehall about the closure of the airport, even though it was perfectly useable for passenger and freight flights, which would have brought investment and jobs into Thanet.

We also made a pledge to oppose a house-building programme to provide 12,000 new homes on green belt land and try to hugely increase population numbers in the area.

What I have learnt from our own mistakes, and certainly those made by the Tories in the Rochester by-election, is that it is imperative to express and justify the party's main policies in local terms. Banging on about extravagance in Brussels will only get you so far in the King's Head. But if you can express the impact of surging, uncontrolled immigration on GP surgeries, primary schools and local wages, then you are making UKIP relevant. Matthew Goodwin's research found that 30 per cent of the British electorate were receptive to UKIP policies, but the absolute key was to try to make them directly relevant. South Thanet will be a real test as to whether, in the last two years, we have managed to hone our message, and whether the programme of better targeting seats has worked.

I reckon that we have a good chance of continuing to dominate Thanet District Council. In May 2013, of eight seats on Kent County Council, we won seven, and the Labour candidate – Scobie – had the other.

My belief that we can be the biggest party in Thanet – certainly on a local level – was not on the basis of some whim or after-lunch emotion. The demographic there really works for UKIP.

Goodwin has pointed out that while Clacton, which we won in the October 2014 by-election, had the best demographic for a UKIP win (a high proportion of blue-collar workers, pensioners, few immigrants and a low number of university graduates), the electoral profile of Thanet was similar, even though it was 143 on our list of target seats. Clacton, by the way, was number one.

Like Rochester, there is an upper-middle-class element in the constituency, but actually it is dominated by a forgotten and long-abandoned working class.

Many in South Thanet struggle. There are a lot of people there earning not a lot of money. Much of the industry that provided local jobs has gone. Few in White-hall care that under two hours from the Commons is a place where people have suffered a series of hammer blows – the closure of coal mines by Thatcher, and Pfizer, the pharmaceuticals giant, selling up and closing their massive research and development facility in Sandwich, costing around 1,500 jobs.

But the fight to win Thanet will not be easy. The 'Hope Not Hate' campaign, which now has no BNP to focus on, has targeted UKIP as their alternative.

We will just have to take what they throw at us, literally. In Rochester, Mark Reckless's UKIP constituency office windows were egged every day in the run-up to the by-election; every day we had to get them cleaned. We are very much expecting to do the same in Thanet. We have a new, larger office due to open that will house the whole Thanet operation, from local council campaigners to activists who are just working on getting the Westminster seat.

We're also expecting a few stunts. Al Murray, the Pub Landlord, announcing that he will stand in South Thanet was one such. It was clearly promotion for his own comedy tour given that within weeks of standing he had spectacularly breached the electoral spending limit of £35,000 by taking out pricey adverts in a number of national newspapers and the London freesheet *Metro*. He will be blocked from standing.

As far back as November, the pollsters Survation conducted a survey, albeit quite a small one, across the constituency. It put Labour in the lead at 35 per cent, UKIP with 30 per cent and the Tories with 28 per cent. Time will tell whether I can swing it, but I do know that this is UKIP's window of opportunity. This is it, we have to do this now. This is my high noon. I remember Andrew Neil, the veteran broadcaster, saying to me just ahead of our European elections win: 'Nigel, most party leaders play down their electoral chances.' I simply replied: 'If I play two more hands of double-or-quits and win, who knows where we could be?'

The party has never had this degree of momentum, or amount of electoral credibility following the European elections win and our two successful by-elections. It has taken me years to turn UKIP into a professional party, to learn how to identify target seats, to discover how to execute an election campaign and to get the vote out.

We have broken every rule in the book and I really hope that it does not stop here.

CHAPTER 9

CARSWELL AND RECKLESS: BY-ELECTIONS AND MAKING HISTORY

THE DAY AFTER the August bank holiday of 2014 was the day that would change my life, and the future of UKIP, forever. It was the day that marked the culmination of plugging away with UKIP for twenty-one years – many in the political wilderness – and would prove once and for all that my mission to drive a party that could take Britain out of the European Union had finally paid off.

What I had not realised on that Tuesday morning was that it would unleash a convulsion in British politics the like of which had not been seen in over thirty years.

It was the day that Douglas Carswell, the Conservative MP for Clacton-on-Sea, a proud and largely poor working-class seaside resort on the Essex coast, would announce that he was dumping the Tory Party and joining UKIP. But, more spectacularly, he also announced that he was resigning his seat in the House of Commons, forcing a by-election. He did this as a matter of honour, declaring that 'the people are my boss'. That sense of honour (and sheer guts) represented a massive departure in how the electorate have come to rightly perceive the arrogance of the British political class.

The by-election he triggered would see one of the biggest political swings since the Second World War and give UKIP its first seat in Westminster.

How fitting that Douglas's announcement was to be made in a Victorian building right opposite the House of Commons in Parliament Square, overlooking the statue of Churchill; that a very British revolution had been triggered outside – not within – the House of Commons, which has not answered or served the people of Britain for years. After that day, no one could ever again call us the joke of British politics.

Douglas's announcement was the culmination of a decade of wooing.

It was Lord (Malcolm) Pearson – the former leader of UKIP and a much-mocked figure by the British media – who had spent the last ten years talking to Eurosceptic MPs in the quiet tea rooms and shabby wine bars of the House of Lords. Malcolm is a deeply knowledgeable and principled peer who was fired by the Conservative Party in 2004 for supporting UKIP in the European elections. And he knew all of the Eurosceptics, including Douglas and Mark Reckless, who followed Douglas to leave the Tories and join UKIP the following month. They all used to meet in the cross-party 'Better Off Out' campaign and Malcolm knew all too well their fears and suspicions about Britain's relationship with Brussels, and Westminster's complicity in it.

Douglas had been thinking about dumping the Conservative Party since the summer of 2013, a year before he jumped ship.

He phoned me at that time on my mobile after we had shared a platform together. He told me how unhappy he was with the Tories and that he distrusted the sincerity of Cameron's recent referendum pledge. I knew straightaway that if Douglas joined us, it would result in a by-election, being the principled and honourable MP that he is. In 2010, UKIP had not bothered to contest Clacton because Douglas Carswell was a fully signed-up member of the 'Better Off Out' campaign. This time would be different. He would be on our side and as an extremely popular constituency MP, there was a good chance Clacton voters would follow him and not the next Tory Cameron chose to stuff there.

After that phone conversation, Malcolm continued to meet Douglas, and Stuart Wheeler, the long-term millionaire donor of UKIP, invited him for lunch. Over the months that followed, Malcolm arranged dinners, mainly in private houses in central London, to try to woo Douglas.

But it was not until the evening of 11 June 2014, at the meeting of the powerful 1922 committee of backbench Tories, that he reached his tipping point. Cameron attended the committee meeting – facing his own enemy – and by all accounts, took a few questions. All of them were about Britain's relationship with Europe. Apparently he then told them that if they wanted to get out of the EU completely, the only party that would deliver an in/out referendum was the Tories. Then he left. That was it; that was supposed to be Cameron's attempt at reassuring his own Eurosceptic MPs – and there are a lot of them – that the Conservative Party was serious about reform in Europe and committed to a referendum.

At that moment, as Cameron strode out of the room (he makes sure that he exits so fast that he doesn't have the inconvenience of having to speak to anyone in his own party), Douglas realised he was going to have to quit and join UKIP. What he did not realise was that his decision – made off the seemingly endless Committee Corridor in the Commons with its flock wallpaper and ghastly patterned carpet – would make political history.

That meeting had left him feeling profoundly let down by Cameron. He believed that Cameron wasn't genuine about re-negotiating Britain's relationship with the EU. He felt Cameron was mouthing platitudes to his own bolshy MPs and that he had no intention of following through. There would be no in/out referendum, no real intention of trying to change the EU Treaty.

Cameron should have known better than to underestimate members of the '22. That committee has skewered plenty of ministers and he should have known that – didn't he read politics, philosophy and economics at Oxford? And didn't he even get a first-class degree? Cameron must have had a suspicion of how powerful they could be – he tried to destroy the committee in May 2010, in a bid to limit how far Tory backbenchers might dare to question compromises he was making to keep the coalition together. Time will tell whether, yet again, it was a meeting of the '22 committee that did for him (as it did for Maggie).

Within a month of that '22 committee meeting – on 8 July – Malcolm and Douglas went for a walk around Victoria Park Gardens, the pretty, small park next to the Lords, overlooking the Thames, just tucked away from Millbank. It is mostly used by early morning dog walkers and the occasional television news crew. It may be within yards of MI5 but, to my knowledge, it was not typically used as a space to plot a convulsion in British politics. During that walk, Douglas told Malcolm that the time had come when he needed to meet me and, provided that I could give him certain assurances, he was ready to jump and join UKIP.

On 24 July, Malcolm, Douglas and I met at a private house at midday in south London.

Douglas needed reassurance that UKIP had the money and the manpower to help him win back Clacton in a by-election – this time with us, rather than the Tories. I was able to give those reassurances and promised absolute confidentiality.

When I left the meeting I was on cloud nine. Not only would the excellent Carswell be joining us, but I felt confident we would win that by-election. As I cabbed my way to Boisdale's restaurant in Belgravia for lunch, I just could not believe it. We were now within weeks of getting our first Westminster seat, and we would finally be on our way. We would be able to draw blood off that lot, the Camerons, the Cleggs, the Milibands – the fools who know nothing of real life, who have never had a job outside the Westminster village and who have happily handed over the running of our country to unelected technocrats in Brussels.

After the meeting, Douglas and I spoke several times on the phone. He was on for it. We had a deal. I wanted to get the announcement out – I was in a hurry to get going – but what delayed us, bizarrely, was that Douglas was on jury service. So we held off. We agreed the Thursday after the August bank holiday, 28 August, would be the day we would unleash what the Tories had had coming to them for years. By then the so-called summer silly season would be over and we could knock the Tories for six on the first day back. I thought that they wouldn't know what had hit them and, as it turned out, they didn't.

Virtually no one knew about Douglas coming to UKIP right up until eleven o'clock on the day when we announced it. In politics, everything leaks, so, if you want to keep a secret, don't tell anyone – or at least tell the fewest people possible. I had not even put the date of my first meeting with Douglas in my diary in case I lost it and it fell into the wrong hands. The only people who knew apart from me, Malcolm and Douglas were Douglas's wife Clementine and my wife Kirsten. Even then, Kirsten only had an inkling because she overheard my phone calls in the kitchen.

I had also told our new treasurer – Andrew Reid – that we were about to incur a very large expenditure but that it was for a good cause. I hinted strongly what it was. Mark Reckless, who was soon to follow Douglas, knew of the move too. But the media team didn't know, and neither did the UKIP top brass.

I told Alex Phillips, my loyal press aide, to book a venue as close to the Houses of Parliament as possible. She chose One Great George Street, the Institute of Civil Engineers, just on the corner of Parliament Square, a rather grand building that backs onto the Cabinet Office and the Treasury. Well, if you are going to plant a political bomb, you may as well hit them where it hurts.

I wanted to make sure the way we announced it was going to be like a jack-in-the-box.

I told the press office that the announcement was about a new donor and invited all of UKIP's senior figures, telling them that we would also be hosting a policy forum. I even managed to persuade Paul Sykes, our long-term party donor, that there was an event in Westminster that I thought he should attend. Sykes was both suspicious and nervous.

I met him the night before in a hotel in central London. Given the amount of support that he had given us, I thought that I should at least give him a heads-up. 'What the hell have you got planned now?' he asked me. He was scared that I was about to lure over some ghastly celebrity who would come out as a UKIP voter, so when I told him it was Douglas, he was delighted.

So there we were: 28 August, just before 11 a.m., as Londoners emerged from the bank holiday weekend. I was standing before a bemused selection of UKIP top figures and even more curious members of the press. Outside the entrance of the Parliament Square building, I made a phone call to Patrick O'Flynn, our head of communications, whom I had told that morning to go and pick up Douglas and bring him to One Great George Street by whatever means possible. But, at two minutes to eleven, I was there but Douglas, however, was not. I phoned Patrick on the mobile: 'Where are you?' I asked. 'I'm 300 yards away,' came the reply. Three minutes passed. Still no Douglas. It felt like I was about to be stood up at the altar.

But he did turn up and, as Malcolm had long predicted, he would keep his word. At that moment, Douglas and I both knew we were about to start to change the course of British politics.

I walked in the room with Douglas and the press looked astonished: the penny had finally dropped. I started by apologising that I had got the media to the event under false pretences – I had told them that I had an important announcement to make, which I then admitted I had not. 'I will, however, hand you over to the Conservative MP for Clacton – Douglas Carswell.'

Douglas then turned to the assembled crowd and began with the words: 'I am today leaving the Conservative Party and joining UKIP.' The UKIP crowd cheered loudly, but most people were just stunned. The real shock, however, was to follow: he said he was resigning as a Member of Parliament and, as a matter of honour, he would stand in a by-election. I looked at our party chairman, Steve Crowther, and my deputy, Paul Nuttall, who were just shaking their heads in disbelief.

Within a few minutes, senior journalists and camera crews started to arrive after seeing the news break on the wires. The venue was so close to the Commons they could run from the so-called 'lobby offices' over the road. The broadcasters and newspapers routinely had only ever sent their B- or C-list reporters on UKIP stories but, as they saw our news, they rapidly sent the A-list to beef up their teams. We were leading the news. The future of UKIP and, by extension, my life, was about to change.

* * *

Barely a month after Douglas said he was joining us, we had another surprise in store for the Conservative Party. This time, however, they were prepared.

The Tory whips spent that month vetting a squad of Conservative Eurosceptics – of whom Mark Reckless was one – demanding an assurance that they were not planning to defect. The ploy was to scare off potential new Kippers and also to threaten that Tory Party central office would be able to publicly brand them as liars if they did quit. It was plain, old-fashioned bullying. But they were bullying because they were scared.

While the resignations of Douglas and later of Mark looked very similar to the outside world, they were in fact completely different from one another.

Firstly, Mark was a very different type of Tory MP from Douglas. Mark had only been an MP for four years, unlike Douglas's term of ten in Clacton; he had a narrower majority and his constituency – on the other side of the estuary from Clacton – had wealthier voters who were more likely to vote Tory than UKIP.

I knew we could win Clacton, but Rochester & Strood had been so far off our radar until Mark said he would join us. Matthew Goodwin had ranked Rochester & Strood as target seat 271 for us. We would be starting from scratch, apart from a few scores of UKIP local party members. And we had under three months to do it before a by-election.

I knew that if Mark left the Conservatives, demanded a by-election and we won Rochester & Strood, it would be high noon for the Tories. Everyone would know that we had eaten into their heartland and it would hurt. It would hurt the party itself, but it would create rumblings about whether Cameron was up to running his own party, and it might encourage others to jump as well. A UKIP win in Rochester was the last thing Cameron needed – and with almost six months between a by-election and the May general election, his world could change quite dramatically.

While Mark and Douglas are very different, their tipping point was the same – the June meeting of the 1922 Committee. Like Douglas, Mark was furious that Cameron appeared to show mere lip service to changing Britain's relationship with Europe. He too felt fobbed off. There was never going to be an in/out referendum under Cameron, was there?

If Douglas could be described as one of the country's most attentive and hard-working constituency MPs, then Mark could well be defined as one of the most rebellious. He was definitely part of the Tory awkward squad, suspicious of Cameron and failing to toe the whips' line on voting for issues such as a rise in university tuition fees and airstrikes on Libya. Mark was also more infamous than famous as an MP as a result of being too drunk to vote on the Budget shortly after he began his term in Parliament. I knew him from Eurosceptic events and, after the drunken episode, I wrote him a letter telling him not to worry. He's completely teetotal now, like Douglas, who hardly touches a drop. God knows what they make of me.

After the June '22 meeting, Mark began to hold regular meetings with a local Medway businessman called John Terry. Douglas had hinted strongly on our 24 July meeting that we should be pursuing Mark. It was another feather in Malcolm's cap.

John Terry was the most important broker between me and Mark. He and John met twelve times between June and August before he made his decision to join us. Mark came twice to see me at my home in Downe, Kent. No lunch, no wine, just pots of tea, and we talked. The first time he came to my home was before Douglas joined, but the second was after and, on that occasion, John drove him there. By then, the campaign to put the frighteners on any Tory looking to join us was so intense, Mark turned up in dark glasses and a baseball cap so that the neighbours wouldn't recognise him. He was convinced that he was being followed, most likely by someone at Conservative central office. It was certainly our suspicion that everyone at UKIP HQ – from me to the press office to the strategists – had their mobiles tapped. Life had become quite surreal. The Tories were getting very scared, and, with it, very, very nasty indeed. It's fair to say Mark was under enormous strain.

On 17 September, Mark had asked one of my campaign organisers, Chris Bruni-Lowe, whether he could arrange a meeting in London between the two of us that night. He was still uncertain. Chris suggested that we meet at his own flat on Cambridge Street in Pimlico – about ten minutes in a cab from the House of Commons. I couldn't get there until about quarter past midnight given that I had been at a dinner. Mark arrived in disguise with a beanie-style woolly hat pulled down over his eyes. We were all slightly paranoid. If the Tories had believed he was on the brink of joining us, they could have thrown him out of the party, thereby discrediting him. I told Mark that he had one chance to really make a difference; he was extremely emotional.

Mark and I had the same conversations as those I had had with Douglas months before. Did we have enough money and people on the ground to run an election campaign and help him win Rochester back? He was putting his career on the line, after all. We knew then that the Tories would throw everything at the Rochester by-election – and they later proved us right. By the end of the meeting, Mark said he was on board.

We decided that the annual UKIP conference in Doncaster on 27 September was the best time to announce it. It would be a few days before the Conservative Party conference, and it would also give us a terrific platform to announce Mark's move.

It was, however, easier said than done. The stage management of the next ten days in the run-up to our party conference was quite phenomenal.

Malcolm, Mark, Chris Bruni-Lowe and I suspected that it was not secure for us to have conversations on our mobile phones. Instead, all of us bought pay-as-you-go mobiles. I have had the same mobile phone number for years, so it wouldn't be difficult to hack it. Once we had the pay-as-you-gos, Mark and I never spoke to each other on our own devices. Mark would call Douglas or Chris and arrange a time when we would be together and they could hand over their phone to talk to Mark. Often, I had to call Mark's wife, Catriona, to speak to him.

Pretty much just like Douglas's announcement, only a very small group of people knew that Mark was preparing to leave the Tories. I didn't tell any of the major donors but once again the treasurer was informed that a large bill was about to land on his desk. He needed to know – by-elections cost us around £100,000 each with the expense of running the local UKIP office, the phone calling, the pamphleteering, the door-to-door campaigning.

On the road with Douglas, campaigning in Clacton, Mark and I agreed the plan for his announcement – while I was standing in a pub car park.

Running my own business and twenty years in politics have taught me is that if you want something really sensitive, really important done, do it yourself. I was not going to take any chances. So, I scouted out the venue of the UKIP conference myself – it was the wonderful Doncaster racecourse within a few miles of Ed Miliband's home. I worked out when my own security team took me there that Gate 8 of the course was the high-security route. I had used the door that was blocked off to conference-goers and press and decided that that had to be Mark's route too. Once Mark was out of the car at the racecourse, he would only have had to walk through two feet of air-lit exposure. I walked the route myself to double-check whether he would be spotted before the announcement. I was taking no chances.

In the days running up to the Doncaster conference day, I called James, my main bodyguard, who is ex-military police, a fellow Kipper and generally an all-round solid bloke. I told him to find a car with darkened windows. On the terrace of the racecourse on the eve of the party conference, I also told one of my security men – Adam Bunny – to collect Chris Bruni-Lowe the next day at 11 a.m., and for both of them to then drive to pick up Mark and bring him to the conference.

Mark and his family were staying at a Center Parcs in Nottinghamshire to keep him well away from the Tories. None of the security chaps had any idea it was Mark who was to be collected. The plan was that Mark would be dropped off, go through the door and wait behind a huge black curtain. Once again, I told Patrick O'Flynn to be in position at 2.30 p.m. backstage. Patrick simply couldn't believe this was happening again.

James was told to lead Mark through the curtain and up to the stage where I would announce him to the near-2,000 Kippers in the conference hall. All I would need was a positive signal to tell me that Mark had arrived.

Before taking the stage, I had told the media that I had a big polling announcement to make. I had also told the UKIP press team that it was going to be a busy afternoon and gave them a wink. I really hoped that they were not planning on any quick, albeit well-deserved, snifters at the racecourse bar, because things were about to go berserk. I called Chris in the car to make sure that Mark was with him, and that was all OK.

Once on stage, I announced the new positive polling, which got the audience going. In Boston & Skegness we were twenty points clear. With this, the crowd was in jubilant mood. I talked through the next few minutes to about forty projected slides and kept milking the applause so I could look stage left. I was trying to catch sight of James there and was desperate to see the thumbs-up from him.

No James, and I was beginning to run out of slides. I began to feel ever so slightly sick and kept peering to my left.

To my enormous relief, James suddenly appeared with a big smile and a thumbs-up. The plan had worked. James and Patrick were with Mark, hiding behind a black Velcro curtain. I stopped the slides and changed tack. Addressing the room, I said: 'I booked a half-hour slot, but I'm done now. So you could go and have a cup of tea or, alternatively, you could listen to a friend of mine who has come to speak to you. He is not a member of our party…'

(Dark murmurs of disapproval emerged from the audience.)

'…he is a Member of Parliament for the Conservative Party. But he is coming to have a chat with our conference this afternoon and I think it will be interesting to hear what he has to say, don't you?'

The penny began to drop. There were cheers.

'Would you please give a warm welcome to Mark Reckless, the Conservative Member of Parliament for Rochester & Strood.'

The audience were on their feet, arms in air, cheering. They knew what was about to happen.

As Mark walked onto the stage, I lifted up my arms to welcome him. The atmosphere was electric. I shook Mark's hand and said to him: 'You're a rock star now.' He looked slightly bewildered in his bookish way, and took the stage, using the same line that Douglas had used a few weeks before.

Mark stood there slightly dazed, but smiling, and turned to address the audience. 'Today, I am leaving the Conservative Party…' The crowd were on their feet again, shouting and cheering. People were in tears and started dancing in the aisles. I don't think I have experienced anything in politics as exciting as that. When the noise subsided, Mark continued: '…and joining UKIP.' With this, the audience went absolutely berserk with a long standing ovation. They began to chant: 'UKIP! UKIP! UKIP!'

I was sitting on the platform next to Steve Crowther, the party chairman, crying with laughter. It was just hilarious.

Mark's speech was truly heartfelt, and the audience knew it: 'These decisions are never easy. There have been many sleepless nights. But this is a decision I make from optimism, a decision that Britain can be better.'

He added:

> People feel ignored, taken for granted, over-taxed, ripped-off and lied to. They have reason to. MPs too often are not their local representatives but agents of a political class. Instead of championing their constituents' interests in Westminster, too often they champion their party's interests in their constituencies. I will resign my seat in Parliament, trigger a by-election and stand for UKIP.

The crowd was on its feet again.

What an absolute coup – and it was all done under the nose of Miliband's constituency within days of the Tory Party conference.

Now we had two Tories joining our ranks. It felt like we were on a roll.

After the euphoria in Doncaster, it did not take long for the venom of the Tories to erupt. Tory bullying of Mark started pretty much immediately. His departure unleashed a volley of abuse. He was an alcoholic, they said. He was a liar and, worst of all, a traitor. Talk about the Nasty Party. The Tories in Rochester tried to put the frighteners on him and his family. It was pure negative American/Australian-style campaigning, led by the Australian Lynton Crosby and the American Jim Messina, both Tory Party strategists. Incessant telephone calls started coming from Washington. Can I prove that the bullying was funded by Conservative central office? No. Do I suspect them? You bet. And it was disgusting.

What it did show, though, is how frightened they were and are. Cameron knew that the Rochester by-election represented high noon. It would be the most important by-election since Shirley Williams and Roy Jenkins fought the SDP by-elections in 1981. He knew that if we won, the very Tories who had turned on Mark would start to turn on him – a leader who could not keep his party united, a leader incapable of leading.

＊　　＊　　＊

So, there we were, finally. Fifteen months on from my first telephone conversation with Douglas – when he told me he was unhappy, suspicious of Cameron and minded to jump ship to UKIP – the two of us are standing in the Clacton-on-Sea UKIP office.

It is 9 September, the morning of the Clacton by-election that would see us get our first Westminster seat. A gloriously sunny day – always good for turn-out – and I'm standing in the back yard of the little office of what was once probably a small shop, having a smoke. Douglas is standing next to me, with a characteristic pink shirt and, uncharacteristically, a tie.

'There's a poll that is putting us on a 6 per cent win today,' I tell Douglas. 'I mean what planet are they on? That lot just don't get it.'

The UKIP office is heaving: volunteers; would-be voters; voters who have already voted; well-wishers; a man from Portsmouth who just wanted to come up for the day; and an excited golden Labrador wearing a UKIP-branded dog warmer. With so many photographers snapping outside, the dog is getting nervous. I know the feeling. It's chaotic, exciting and, frankly, extraordinary.

There is something vicar-like about Douglas. I just didn't realise people like him still existed – a true gentleman, with real poise and care. It is no surprise to learn that his father was a doctor in Uganda, the first person to diagnose HIV there. And there is something of the missionary about Douglas.

Walking around Clacton, constituents greet him and not only does he know their name, he knows their husband's or wife's name. When he first quit the Tories, a man shouted at him in the street: 'Good on you, mate, what took you so f**king long!' There are constituencies across the country where people don't even know the name of their MP, let alone what they look like. He makes the point that he serves the constituents of Clacton, not the party whips in Westminster, and the people of Clacton know it. At a political debate at a local school a few weeks earlier, hosted by Douglas and me, a woman stood up as soon as we opened questions to the floor. 'What', she asked, 'are you going to do about the fact that austerity cuts have meant that we have no street lighting after midnight? My son was stabbed, and is dead, because the streets of Clacton are so dangerous.' The atmosphere changed.

What on earth do you say to a grieving mother?

Douglas already knew her. As he started to answer her, it was clear he had visited her home, knew all about her son and was helping her campaign to stop knife crime. How many other MPs have such engagement at grass-roots level? I thought him to be extraordinary.

In the old days of UKIP, polling day used to consist of a lunch and I had always felt like a spare part. We used to think that there was nothing to do, that we had done all the campaigning we could and so the best way forward was to find a restaurant, get the wine list, try not to drink too much and wait for the count.

We have grown up a lot since then. In Clacton, we had been developing a voter database for months. It had the names of 5,000 households across the constituency on it. Of them, we knew which were undecided, which of them said they were likely to vote UKIP, and those who were die-hard Kippers. A UKIP activist – Ron Reeves, a retired builder – had organised the UKIP team in Jaywick.

He had been leading a team since before the European elections in May, going door to door across the constituency, talking to them about UKIP and asking about their worries. Some of the homes he went back to three or four times over the summer. So, by the time I went out on the stump on 9 September with party volunteers, armed with lists of households, they were able to tell me: 'No, not that house, Nigel – you need to go to No. 31.' It was forensic, and it worked. To be honest, it reminded me of the City – they just knew their market.

Clacton is a real mix. Right on the Essex coast, it used to be where working-class people from the East End of London would take their summer holidays, some of whom would then retire there with a bungalow and a small garden. Frinton is the upmarket end of Clacton: a classic, Victorian seaside resort – grand hotels, beach huts, bowls clubs and very handsome properties. Clacton town itself is less prosperous. It is packed with immaculate bed and breakfasts, amusement arcades, Toby restaurants and chippies.

And at the poorer end are areas such as Jaywick, which frankly have just been completely abandoned by Westminster. A government report a few years ago on social deprivation found that Jaywick was the poorest town in Britain. The report was clearly pointless, because from what I can see, nothing has been done to improve their lot since it came out.

James drove me to Jaywick to chivvy the vote, encourage people to get out and get to the polling booths. It was my eighth trip to Clacton. I love pavement politics, going house to house. Blair abandoned all of this sort of thing, of course. New Labour wasn't about speaking to the electorate, knocking on doors and asking them to vote for you. That would have been too demeaning for that lot. Pavement politics was replaced by sound bites, spin and pre-records.

I remember walking down a street called Standard Avenue. Well, perhaps the word 'street' isn't accurate. A street would imply that the residents who live there had a road. They don't. The residents of Standard Avenue have to suffer the indignity of basically living off a track with massive holes, around which they have to navigate their cars. The council have clearly let them down – there is rubbish everywhere. People fear crime – garage doors are padlocked and CCTV cameras have been installed on the sides of houses. Fat lot of good that will do if there is no street lighting after midnight. And in the surrounding streets, prefabs are common. They were built as an emergency measure during the war, for goodness sake. If you want a real example of how Westminster no longer cares about the electorate it is supposed to represent, it is Jaywick. How weird though, that I am campaigning in a safe Tory seat, for a former Tory candidate, but Jaywick is a Labour ward.

Jaywick people are a proud lot but the Westminster crowd certainly didn't want to be seen with them on polling day. I saw a few teenagers wearing a Tory rosette there, looking a bit lost, but that was it – they didn't have a clue. The Conservatives had not done the legwork and it was too late. As I went from house to house, I asked: 'Have you had Labour down here?' Most said no. No one bothered with them.

I rang the door at one house, in a neat cul-de-sac full of pastel-coloured two- or three-bedroomed houses, and a man in his twenties answered. 'Hey, Nigel. I've met you before. In Somerset. At the floods.' It was astonishing. I meet tens of thousands of people, but I still find it amazing that I would bump into someone in that way. There were houses with purple posters in the front room window declaring 'I'm voting for Carswell' and properties with pro-UKIP election posters in their front gardens.

I had not bargained on the fury against Labour – and by people I assumed were once their core vote. One man ran up to me, shouting: 'F**k Labour! Go and kick them up the backside, Nigel!'

Others came out of their houses, or as they were getting

out of their cars: 'Nigel, no need to worry … I've already voted. I voted for you!' It was 11 a.m. and they had already been out to vote.

I was on a roll. What a high. I knew we were within hours of making history. The last two decades were about to pay off. It was all a bit surreal and became even more weird when, checking my messages in the back of the Land Rover (I get 300 texts on busy days), I saw something that quite frankly will stay with me to the end. A rather stocky horse – I would later discover his name was 'Shadow' – was trotting along the streets of Clacton with an enormous UKIP flag emblazoned across his rump, as his rather lovely rider, called Sheila, took him out for their late morning hack. 'Stop the car!' I told James. I just had to get out. I ran over the road to speak to her. How often does your party connect with someone in that way?

It was clear to me all day though: as much as 9 September was – from now on – going to effectively be my second birthday, it was not my day, but Douglas's. It belonged to him. He had had the guts to jump ship and it was about to pay off.

So I decided, while he was canvassing, to try to keep a lower profile until we got to the count.

A few of us went to the pub. As any politician will tell you: pace yourself on polling day, because it is going to be a long one. The count can go into the early hours and on this one I would certainly have to do live TV, both straight after the vote and first thing for the breakfast shows.

We arrived at The Wick pub with a few advisers. It was perfect: it had a polling station along the side of it and was run by, and full of, Kippers. A young couple were sitting in silence near me and the team, with their Staffordshire Bull Terrier. They said nothing to us, and I was conscious that we might have been interrupting their lunch. But, as we pulled out of the car park, the man dashed over to the Land Rover. 'God bless you, Nigel. You smoke. I smoke. I am a total sinner. But we are the silent majority, and we're not so silent now.'

He said 'we'. I liked that. After twenty-one years in the wilderness, it was no longer just 'me'. The party was about 'us', and it felt very good indeed.

Back to the Douglas campaign trail. With him,

campaigning was never going to involve a pub. Instead, followed by broadcasters and the press, he took me somewhere that I have not been for at least twenty years – a McDonald's. It was mayhem. Douglas queued up behind baffled teenagers and ordered two McFlurries. I still have no idea what one is. Douglas handed me the pot of ice-cream with a stick in it. Was I supposed to drink it or smoke the stick thing? He is a massive fan of them, Lord help him. Ad vans appeared and we both climbed onto the side of them. It was huge fun. You wouldn't have had Miliband or Cameron jumping onto one of those things. They are so out of touch, so buttoned up, I don't think either of them has really had any fun for years.

Just as we were preparing to leave, Alan 'Howling Laud' Hope, leader of the Monster Raving Loony Party, turned up. He is fantastic in his white tuxedo, round tummy and big hat. I have known him for years and he is great. All of the Loonies vote UKIP. One was bearing a placard in Clacton declaring: 'We are against placards with pointless slogans'. I once had a chat with him when he appeared to be very low. When I asked him what was wrong he decried the fact that some of his party members were actually *canvassing*. 'They should just be laughing,' he said, despairingly. Neither of us could stop laughing.

At that point, my team and I, which included Andrew Reid, went to our hotel just outside Clacton for egg and cress sandwiches and pots of tea. It was going to be a long night. I went for a steam and a swim, a few Tanqueray and tonics, then dinner. By 11 p.m. we were off for the count in Clacton town hall, which was surrounded by protesters. I know it was late, but some of the Tories and the Labour camp were wandering around in a daze. They had no idea what was about to happen to them.

But, to be fair, we had no idea what was about to happen to us either. At about the same time that we arrived at the hall to meet Douglas, my phone rang.

Three hundred miles north, on the outskirts of Manchester, another political bomb was about to detonate. In the parallel by-election of Heywood & Middleton, the UKIP vote was being counted and it was clear that it was going to be a very close call between Labour and UKIP. Very close indeed. Sure, I was keeping my eye on the Clacton vote, but the real story of the night had already moved on. We were taking the Labour vote by storm up north – in a constituency disgusted by the sex abuse scandal in children's homes there, covered up by the local Labour council. We had a very strong candidate in Heywood: John Bickley – tall, very well turned-out, brought up in a council house in Langley.

Even up until the weekend before Clacton and Heywood, the polls were putting us twenty points behind in the north Labour seat. I know from being on the wrong side of too many deals in the City that you simply can't count your chickens, but I had thought the polls had got us wrong, that we might do better than they anticipated. But I had never dared believe it would be this close. The UKIP office in Heywood called back. We lost the constituency by just 623 votes. 623 votes! We were demanding a recount. It was dizzying. Had we won Heywood, it would have been the political equivalent of Krakatoa. Why on earth hadn't we pushed harder there? Campaigned more? One more push and we might have won it. Yet, I was thrilled that we had properly scared Labour.

The Clacton vote came in at about 3 a.m. Out of an electorate of 61,000 people, 51.2 per cent voted. Of those, 21,113 voted for Douglas – which means UKIP netted 67 per cent of the ballot. It was one of the biggest swings since the Second World War. The Tories came in with 8,709; Labour 3,957; and the Liberal Democrats, bless them, limped home with 483 votes. It was clear to me even then that the Labour vote had been propped up by very angry Liberal Democrats and that they had disguised the real damage that had been inflicted on Labour that night.

Standing in front of the stage in Clacton town hall, listening to Douglas's characteristically dignified acceptance speech, I looked up at the coat of arms above his head, with the legend: '*Lux Salubritas et Felicitas*' – 'Light, Health and Happiness'. Couldn't have put it better myself.

We left quickly after the vote and went back for the victory party at The Wick pub. It was packed with Kippers and a huge cheer erupted as we walked in, victorious. I had three pints lined up in front of me before I even got to the bar (which I jumped over). The atmosphere was electric. But, as well as the sheer exhaustion and dizzy elation, I had a moment to think. In this proud Anglo-Saxon town, long ago discarded by the Westminster political class, something amazing had happened. The Anglo-Saxons had a view of life – that it is a bird that flies from the darkness into the warmth and community of the mead hall, then back into the blackness. That night in Clacton, as we entered the victory party, UKIP was finally alive – and it had a future. We were flying into the mead hall.

For the first time, the results of Clacton and Heywood were proof that we could draw blood off the Tories and Labour at the same time. In the early hours of 10 September, I knew that no one could ever again define us as a flash-in-the-pan protest party, a vehicle for disaffected, well-heeled Tories who hated Brussels. I know that we used to be a sort of Kingsley Amis party, full of angry old men, but not now. I also knew that within a few hours I would be on the *Today* programme and doing the other breakfast television shows, and that they would say we were just a protest party. But protest parties do not get 60 per cent of the vote – rarely do they get more than 16 per cent. We proved that night that we had broad appeal. And we were on our way. A very British – and very purple – revolution had begun.

*   *   *

There is a plaque opposite the UKIP office in the main street in Rochester. It reads: 'XXIX miles to London Bridge'. As I stood outside the office, on a charming street full of charity shops, tea rooms and Christmas decorations, I really hoped it was an omen. I longed for that plaque to mean 29 miles to Westminster.

The by-election of Rochester & Strood was so important it was terrifying. And while all the polls had us properly ahead on that Thursday morning of 20 November, I still felt sick. The stakes were just enormous. If we lost this one, the Tories could try to argue that we were a damaged, one-seat wonder. If we lost this, those contemplating jumping ship to UKIP might think twice and stay put instead.

Then there were the donors to think about. There was a lot of money riding on us winning Rochester. Clacton,

Heywood & Middleton, Rochester and the Rotheram police commissioner campaigns cost us around £400,000. We had bet the bank on the lot. Without a Rochester win, how could I convince any future backers that we were worth funding? They could say, quite reasonably, that Clacton was always going to be ours but that, when it came down to it, we couldn't cut the mustard in a constituency that was not home turf. Basically, if we lost Rochester, how could I say we could compete with any dignity or success in the general election six months later? Rochester was also going to be where UKIP would have to fight the absolute colossus of the Conservative Party – their money, their size, their dirty tricks. I knew they would throw the kitchen sink at winning Rochester, but it would be a few hours before I quite realised just what that meant.

The whips had already insisted that every Tory MP visit Rochester & Strood three times between September and November. Ministers had their quota too. Pity the poor constituents. Would you really want that lot trampling around in your neighbourhood, poking their noses in, permanently wishing they were somewhere else?

As I awoke at 5 a.m., as usual, on that crisp, bright morning, I realised that most days from now until the May general election were going to be like this. Imagine that. Every day counts. Every day is critical. It was mind-blowing. To say I was apprehensive would be an understatement.

But what was reassuringly familiar, as James and I travelled in the Land Rover just half an hour to Rochester from my home in Downe, was that I was on home ground.

Rochester is very well known to me: both of my sons went to prep school there, my half brother and sister-in-law live near Rochester and my aunt and uncle were married in Rochester Cathedral. I have strong links all over Kent.

The campaigning that I had done in Rochester & Strood in the two months since Mark had said he was joining UKIP was tough, but it had brought back some extremely happy memories.

Both my boys, Sam and Tom, who are my sons from my first marriage, went to King's Rochester school. While it was a period that coincided with my divorce from their mother Clare, they were still happy times. Still working in the City, my Saturday lunchtimes were often spent picking them up for the weekend, stuck in the interminable school-related traffic in Rochester, only to ferry them back on Sunday evening. It was also when I learnt how to cook – well, I couldn't take them for a curry every Saturday night.

The centre of Rochester town is glorious, with beautiful narrow streets, the spectacular eleventh-century cathedral and, around it, buildings that date back from the fourteenth century to Charles Dickens's time.

In the nine trips I had made to Rochester between Mark joining UKIP and by-election day, my nervousness about the political feat that lay before us was weirdly tempered by memories of the boys at school. To get to the UKIP office, at the foot of the cathedral, you have to drive past my boys' old boarding house – Salis – where they both lived as weekly boarders and had cricket nets in the evening. I used to drink in the pub opposite their school house – the Coopers Arms – waiting for them.

Not everyone in Rochester was as lucky as my boys.

A lot of the constituency was hit hard after the power

station closed, courtesy of an EU directive, and a rapidly rising Eastern European population has put untold pressure on local schools, GP surgeries and wages. The Royal Engineers' presence has long gone, as has the navy. There are a few boatyards and rope-makers but, in short, if you can't get a job in London (it's about half an hour on the train), then you have to try to make ends meet setting up your own business or working for one. There is no industry here. The beautiful properties around the cathedral and the castle quickly become run-down streets with poor lighting and few amenities. And once through those areas, Rochester quickly becomes rural, and rural poor at that.

For the Tory fools who were ordered to visit Rochester in the run-up to the by-election, it must have been quite an education – for much of this part of the Medway, Westminster has long forgotten.

Even though the constituency boundaries were changed, the charismatic Labour QC Bob Marshall-Andrews had won the seat in 1997, 2001 and 2005. It took Mark ten years to win it for the Conservatives. He moved his family down there to try to secure the constituency, and then finally he won it in 2010 with a good majority of 9,000. After just four years, though, he gave it all up and risked losing the seat running for UKIP. It was a very real risk. And a gutsy one for him to take. I took heart, though, that the Medway has been marginal since 1945; it has always swung across the political spectrum, I think because the demographic is so mixed.

But even with all this in mind, we would have a fight on our hands to win it. I knew once Mark indicated that he might jump ship that winning Rochester would be tough because we were starting from scratch. Prior to Mark joining us, we had no data on any of the constituents, no real People's Army on the ground, not even a UKIP office. All we had were a few UKIP activists. Mark made his final decision to quit in Chris's flat in the early hours of 18 September. The by-election was on 20 November. That left us two months to cover an entire constituency, and win. And everyone in Westminster – the political class and the media alike – wanted to watch us fail.

In the two months we had to win Rochester, Chris Bruni-Lowe had a critical role. We pushed on a number of fronts. First, we tried to build a massive profile in Rochester. I cleared my diary, making nine trips to the constituency in eight weeks. We hosted two public debates there, and got our so-called People's Army out and knocking on doors, communicating with voters. Second, we used the software that we had used so effectively in the Clacton by-election. From the data we collected from our door-to-door campaigners, we were able to build a database that recorded who were definite UKIP voters, the might-bes and the definite nos. We had thousands of names on that database. Our tight campaign did not go unnoticed, as Matthew Goodwin wrote just before the by-election in the *Daily Telegraph*. In his article, he said that our campaign was disciplined and far from amateur.

By the time we got to the office, it was, as usual, election-day mayhem. In the front of the office, there was, naturally, a dog wearing a UKIP dog warmer. It always seems to be a golden Labrador. The office was packed with Kippers and outside was chocker with camera crews, photographers and party volunteers. Through the back were three tiny rooms, a lavatory and a back yard where I could have a smoke and grab private phone calls with Alex, Patrick and Sykes. Hardly the West Wing. As I walked into the back office, Chris Bruni-Lowe was sitting hunched over a computer in one of the tiny offices, crunching voting data. Chris had for years worked for Eurosceptic MPs running referendum campaigns on Britain's membership of the EU, but then switched to work for us when he moved with Douglas Carswell. I then gave him the role within UKIP of helping devise and manage the voter database.

By 11.30 that morning, Chris told me 3,700 had already voted for us. We knew, however, that we had to play Rochester differently from Clacton on polling day.

Unlike the Clacton by-election a month earlier, Rochester constituents had been inundated with pamphlets, campaigners and calls from all of the parties. By the time polling day arrived, our activists had been told that Rochester constituents were pig sick of politicians and wanted to be left alone. If you were unlucky, you'd get a handful of Tory MPs ringing your bell and Conservative Party central office phoning you at home. If you were really, really unlucky you'd get Cameron beaming at you on your doorstep. I had no plans on bothering people again during the day. So, instead, I decided to chivvy the troops and go to the polling stations.

We drove to a school for severely disabled children, which for the day was host to a polling station. Usually the tellers are so bored they welcome having anyone to talk to. This time, they barely had time for pleasantries they were so busy. It was heaving – people were coming out in force. I lit another cigarette, calmed down and cheered up.

I love being out and about, talking to people, especially on election day. And of the thirty or so polling stations we visited, I got chirpier. Labour hadn't even bothered to send a representative to any of those I went to; there was a sprinkling of Lib Dems, but the place was crawling with Tories. Seeing the might of the Conservative Party when they choose to hit back is intimidating – they really have the resources, and it made me nervous.

But one of the best things about politics is the people you meet. I used to meet amazing (and bonkers) people in commodities trading, but it is nothing compared to the sheer variety of people you meet in politics. And the Rochester & Strood by-election was no exception.

Pulling up to the polling station at the Hoo Ness Yacht Club, just on the Medway, was Charlie, an old friend who had joined UKIP in 1999 and still actively campaigned for us. He was part of the backbone of our People's Army. 'What time does your shift finish, Charlie?' I asked, eyeing my watch and noting that it was only just lunchtime. 'Ten tonight, when the polls shut,' he said, beaming. 'Go and see the wife, she's asleep in the green Volvo down the road.'

Hoo is prime Thatcher territory. Maggie had made real inroads there, what would have been thirty years ago; the classic Tory working-class vote: semi-detached homes, small gardens, a village hall and a few shops. Around from the yacht club are tiny roads of neat prefabs, none of which have mains gas.

Having done a round of the polling stations, a small group of us popped to the pub for a few pints and some sandwiches. Then back to the media circus. Down the Rochester high street was an old-fashioned sweetshop, whose owner had very cleverly run his own political poll, displayed in the front window. We were at 48 per cent – comfortably in the lead. Every other party had visited it and now it was my turn. Through the scrum of thirty or so photographers, TV crews and reporters outside, I went in to buy my bag of rhubarb and custard bonbons, which I used to eat as a boy. The atmosphere was mad, electric and terrifically exciting. As I turned to the counter, I recognised the shop assistant – a young woman called Megan who had been at school with my eldest son. Then onto canvassing. It was early evening, dark and cold.

By six o'clock that evening, Chris Bruni-Lowe finally gave me the news I had been waiting for. Having seen the force of the Tories, I had thought that we would win but suspected by a much slimmer majority. I had been so nervous I was taking antacids. But then, Chris told me, according to our data, we were home and dry. We had Rochester.

Instead of celebrating just yet, I remembered my father telling me that one election year he had decided not to vote on polling day but, late on, just before the polling stations were due to close, a Tory Party activist had knocked on his door. He said that he felt if they had bothered to traipse round his neighbourhood, then he should make the effort to vote. It was with that in mind that we visited Cuxton, where many properties there overlook the River Medway.

It was a classic Tory area – some of the houses were very pricey. Between 5 p.m. and 7 p.m. that evening, high up above the Medway in the pitch black, we used the voting data sheets to knock on the doors of the undecided. Scrabbling up and down people's steep garden steps, and slipping on the driveways, made me realise one of the reasons I love politics. Ronald Punt, a retired chap, was one of my favourites: 'Already voted for you, Nigel. Then had a round of golf. Where's your pint?'

Another couple who had both voted UKIP that day told me that they had written to Mark on the day he resigned, praising his integrity and saying: 'They [other MPs] call themselves "the Honourable".' Another man told us he had voted Tory for the last ten years but had changed to UKIP that day. I turned up on the doorstep of one well-appointed bungalow and a man opened the front door and immediately told me to wait: 'You're about to make my wife's day,' he said. His wife ran to the front door and threw her arms round me squealing with delight. 'I've always wanted to meet you! It's been such a strange day: I've just had Iain Duncan Smith on the phone asking me to vote Conservative.' Extraordinary.

When we returned to the UKIP office for an update on voting, one of the party activists warned me: 'Careful, Nigel. There are loonies out there,' pointing at the street outside. To which, I replied: 'You mean Alan? I must go and see him.' Alan 'Howling Laud' Hope is the leader of the Monster Raving Loony Party and I have always liked him, not least because they all vote UKIP. They are also tremendous fun. As we chatted in front of the cameras – me with my Bayeux tapestry tie, him in his white tuxedo and cowboy hat – a well-wisher shouted: 'Good luck, Nigel!', to which Alan, with faux petulance replied: 'What about me?' It was priceless.

The businessman John Terry, who had been one of Mark's supporters, hosted a dinner for UKIP activists and me, after which we headed for the count. It was unbelievably slow. Mark turned up at 12.30 a.m. and the result came in at 4.55 a.m.

The returning officer announced that Mark had bagged 16,867 votes, ahead of the Conservatives, who got 13,947. It was far from a landslide, but Rochester belonged to us.

Mark gave a very dignified speech, thanking, among others, the Labour voters who had joined the UKIP revolution. He pointed out that UKIP, not Labour, now speaks to the working man and woman.

I went to bed. For forty-two minutes. Then came the media. I couldn't wait for the moment to tell them of our success. We had carefully choreographed the following day. Mark did some media, then was straight on the 7.42 a.m. train to London to take part in the NHS debate in the Commons but, for the first time, as a UKIP MP. He was the first MP in sixty years to return to work as an MP the next day. It felt right – not only was his mother a nurse and his father a doctor, it was the signal that it put out: we were back to work.

Without a doubt, winning Rochester & Strood was one of the proudest moments of my life.

CHAPTER 10

MAY 2015: THE NEXT BIG STEP

FROM WHERE I am sitting now, in my small office in Brooks Mews at the back of Claridge's hotel, I am certain of one thing.

With just a few months to go till the general election of 2015, this is the most unpredictable election for 100 years.

I remember saying to Andrew Neil, the presenter of the BBC *Sunday Politics* show, 'You may as well fire all of those experts you have sitting on your sofas talking about the election, because they have as much chance of predicting the outcome as I have playing pin the tail on the donkey.'

This election is completely uncertain and its uncertainty is largely because of UKIP and the Scottish National Party (SNP). Any gains that the SNP makes will be at the expense of the Labour Party in Scotland and any real gains that UKIP makes will be at the expense of all three parties: the Conservatives, Labour and the Liberal Democrats. UKIP has upset the political apple cart, and I am constantly asked how many seats UKIP can win in May. My public answer mirrors my private view: I just don't know, and no one else has a clue either.

Are we going to win a handful of seats? Yes. Could we surprise everyone, including ourselves? Yes. I was astonished by a poll that put UKIP in the lead in Cannock Chase, Staffordshire – we are making inroads in places we simply had not expected. Are we in with a sporting chance of getting enough seats to make a difference? Perhaps. But from where I am sitting now, the likelihood of Britain waking up to something that resembles a loose three-party coalition, rather than a two-party one, is pretty high, I would say.

Depending on how many seats UKIP gets, I could see the Tories, UKIP and the Democratic Unionist Party (the DUP in Northern Ireland) doing some kind of deal. I do not foresee a Labour victory – their campaign is in too much trouble in Scotland and the north of England.

Labour simply has no clear message. If you ask a voter what the Labour Party is for, you would struggle to get an answer. It has little clear purpose and its policies, as far as you can identify them, are not that far from those of the Conservatives. Although I did get Miliband wrong – I had long thought that he would change Labour's position on Europe; I now accept I was wrong – he is as dead-set on the EU project as Clegg. As for the trade unions that fund Labour, they have also changed their identity: now they are in favour of corporatism and supporting the concept of big government, taking choices and control away from their members. The unions support open-door immigration and endorse the whole EU project. It seems to matter little to them that one of the consequences of uncontrolled immigration is that the mass of cheap foreign labour on our shores undercuts local wages for British workers. In some sectors – such as construction and local household services – the minimum wage has effectively become the maximum wage. Trade unions have a proud history of acting for the interests of their members, of championing employee rights on issues such as pay and fairness. Do they do so now? Only the late Bob Crow, the leader of the National Union of Rail, Maritime and Transport Workers, seemed to me to stand up for the interests of the working man.

The trade union movement in the 1970s finished the Heath government on issues such as the planned closure of coal-fired power stations. Yet when the Kingsnorth power station in Kent was shut in March 2013, courtesy of the EU Large Combustion Plants Directive, there was no opposition from the unions at all. A hundred people – in what is a pretty depressed area of Kent – lost their jobs, but there was not a peep out of the unions. Both Labour and the unions have just lost their way – and it's no wonder with the sheer paucity of talent within their ranks.

The Labour Party has lost so much ground over the last ten years. Under the Blair project, the party had some incredibly talented people: Tony Blair, Alastair Campbell and Peter – now Lord – Mandelson were, and are, extraordinarily impressive politicians. Who does Labour have now? Some bloke from Washington called David Axelrod. For sure, he oversaw the presidential campaign that saw Barack Obama get into the White House in the elections of 2008, even though he would turn out to be a very poor and ineffective president. But the kind of negative campaigning that he espoused, that is supposed to have been such a success, has driven down American turn-out to about 50 per cent.

Both the Tories and Labour are going down the American route of negative campaigning, which I think many British voters find tawdry. It's a turn-off to see politicians from rival parties ripping each other apart. In my campaigning in Ramsgate in the run-up to the general election, I found as many people saying that they used to be Labour supporters as I did people saying that they used to be Tories.

Cameron said in his annual conference speech: if you go to bed with Farage on election night, you will wake up with

Miliband. His point was that if a Tory switched his allegiance from the Conservative Party to UKIP, it would have the effect of simply denying Cameron a majority. But he was proven wrong by the Rochester & Strood by-election in November 2014. UKIP won a 42 per cent share of the vote – and that was for a constituency we'd designated as No. 271 on our list of target seats… After that, in Rochester, if you voted UKIP, you got UKIP.

No, from where I am now, I think that the Tories will be the biggest party when we wake up on Friday 8 May. But I suspect they will be damaged because they have lost so much of the blue-collar vote and are just banking on the ageing middle classes to back them. Because of this, a Tory majority, I believe, is improbable at best.

The Liberal Democrat vote will collapse. Nick Clegg will be lucky to keep his Sheffield seat, and overall as a party they will be lucky to keep a third of the fifty-seven seats they won in 2010. Then they bagged 23 per cent of the vote. They won't get anywhere near that this time round. It is an extraordinary irony that the party that supports the electoral system of proportional representation (PR) will benefit from the British first-past-the-post system. In the European elections, which are conducted on PR lines, they were pretty much wiped out. They ended up with just one seat.

The Greens will get nothing, thank goodness. For all of the guff from Caroline Lucas, the former leader of the Green Party, there is no resurgence of the Green movement. The reality is that the party is very badly organised, and their claim that they are enjoying a surge in membership is questionable at best. There are holidays to Portugal being advertised where part of the package is free membership to the Green Party whether you want it or not, for goodness sake. I reckon that Lucas will lose her seat – Brighton Pavilion – the only Westminster seat that the Greens have. They have been appalling at running the local authority in Brighton – they have one of the worst recycling records in the country, supposedly one of their mainstay policies. The police there refuse to enforce their daft 20 mph road speed policy. It is chaos.

As for me? I face my own challenge in winning South Thanet – a challenge that Miliband and Cameron do not face with their safe seats. And I have to do it while leading the national party. I think I will win the seat – we have been fighting quietly under the radar, holding public debates, conducting a campaign that is micro-targeting ward by ward, and I think that we are gaining real momentum.

The arithmetic says that the Tories will be the biggest party in May 2015, but that it may be so squeaky they will need the support of two other parties to get the numbers up and ensure, for example, that they can get their Budget through.

I see a Tory, UKIP, Democratic Unionist Party (DUP) three-way deal as a possible scenario, where UKIP and the Northern Irish would take a similar role to that of the Liberal Democrats now. Given that Cameron has about 100 rebellious Tory backbenchers to deal with, it strikes me that they would not want to do another deal with the Liberal Democrats. Those backbenchers were on our side on a number of issues – both foreign and domestic. Many of them were on our side on the Syria vote – they, like us, simply did not want to get drawn into military intervention in the Middle East. And that same Tory awkward squad are similarly Eurosceptic and against an open-door immigration policy.

I suspect the first obstacle to doing a deal with UKIP for the Tories is pride. They have a long history of being perfectly beastly about UKIP. When Grant Shapps – the Tory Party chairman (I cannot keep a straight face when I hear his name and title expressed in the same sentence) – said that they would never do a deal with us, he just didn't realise that it doesn't work like that. It is all about the numbers. It will be complicated, but the DUP have eight seats now before the May election, and that is likely to rise next time round. They too have a Eurosceptic position – like UKIP. UKIP and the DUP have a mutual respect for each other even though we are rivals. They have moved on from their sectarian approach to things.

Every government needs to know that they have the numbers to get their Budget passed and if it were between a deal with me and the DUP or a deal with the Liberal Democrats, I know which way I would go. If the numbers work as I think, there would be two scenarios. First, would

UKIP wish to form a formal coalition with the Tories? The answer is no. We are radicals; we want real change to help Britain get back self-governance and self-confidence. There are many other areas where we can make a contribution. But I have no desire to swap the short-term privilege of a ministerial car for everything that we have fought for. If the numbers worked, I would look to do a deal where we would back key votes for them – such as the Budget – but in return for very specific criteria on an EU referendum.

2015 is just the beginning of the journey for UKIP. I am already thinking of 2020. I genuinely believe that UKIP can be a very major party in that election, but not if our voters think we have sold out.

I have no desire to sit around the Cabinet table in No. 10, no desire to have a ministerial title and absolutely no desire to swap the chance to get Britain out of the EU for some grandee position in government.

I have never had a business card with a title on it, largely because I have never wanted or needed a title. I know whether I am doing well or badly – I don't need that kind of recognition. It just isn't my kick.

Apart from anything else, most of the people sitting around that Cabinet table are ghastly – I do not want to be with them and I am sure they feel the same way about me. I have only been through the doors of No. 10 once, when I was invited there in the 1990s – and once is enough.

The terms of my deal would be very precise and simple.

I want a full and fair referendum to be held in 2015 to allow Britons to vote on being in or out of the European Union. There is to be no wiggle room for 're-negotiation' somewhere down the line.

I have four criteria.

1. Timing is key. The EU is facing an existential crisis and, given that it only takes a few weeks to launch a referendum, it should be held in 2015.

2. The wording of the question that will be put to voters. 'Do you wish to be a free, independent sovereign democracy?' This would be a starting point. You only have to look at the wording of the referendum question

in the Scottish independence vote to see that the 'yes' side was initially conceded to Alex Salmond. The wording of the question matters terribly. In 1975, the referendum question was so loaded, it afforded a great deal of wiggle room. Then Britain was asked to vote on whether we should stay in the European Economic Community; the question was: 'Do you think Britain should stay in the European Community?' Just over 67 per cent said yes.

3. Third is eligibility. Who gets to vote? It is my strong belief that the four million EU citizens living in the UK without British passports should not be allowed. And yes, that does include my German wife. They are eligible to vote in European elections but they should not have the right to decide on Britain's future in the EU. It may be that that would require us to do battle with the European Court of Justice – but so be it.

4. Fourth is information and funding. I saw how the Irish referendums were conducted. There were large amounts

of literature disseminated that purported to be legitimate campaigning. I would want strict spending limits so that neither side is able to outspend the other – no shenanigans. For me to play ball with Cameron, I would also want an ombudsman to police coverage of the referendum – both the campaigning and the day itself – to make sure that there was even coverage from all sides – even though the BBC will hate it.

If Cameron agrees to those terms, provided that the Tories show that they are being responsible about the Budget and that they are committed to deficit reduction, there is no question that UKIP would not do a deal.

It is difficult to see at this point who we could have a conversation with among the Tories – a vast number of them hate us and I dislike them. But there are a few – Michael Gove, the now Chief Whip of the Conservatives, for example – that I have always been friends with. Most of them are so negative, but he has always been the most civil. I would trust him across the table.

The DUP – should they too want to do a deal and be in

a position to – would probably want to offer their loyalty in return for more Whitehall money to be invested in Northern Ireland, but I cannot speak for them.

None of us – the British voter, the media luvvie, the policy wonk, or the party leader – know what 8 May 2015 is going to look like. I think it will reveal new evidence of what we have all seen during the last eighteen months – a convulsion in British politics.

The last eighteen months have changed my life. From my back operation that prevented me from becoming disabled to winning the European elections in May 2014 and then the two by-elections that we won. This is our time.

The excitement of this period has been extraordinary. UKIP has taken on the political establishment and given them a run for their money. We have rumbled their complacency and, with the issue of uncontrolled immigration, changed the terms on which this 2015 election will be fought. I have learnt so much – chiefly that the higher up you go, the fewer people you can trust. This journey has increasingly become lonely.

I desperately want UKIP to do well and to change the face of British politics, but I am also a realist – careers of politicians are often slow in the making and rapid in the ending. That's the nature of the game, the fascination of it. I have learnt one other thing, however, that neither Cameron, Miliband nor Clegg have grasped: politics is about people – the absolute spectrum of the very worst to the very best.

So over to you, dear voter. It is all down to you now.

ACKNOWLEDGEMENTS

WOULD LIKE, FIRST and foremost, to thank Suzy Jagger for all of her hard work on this book.

Thanks also go to all the working men and women who have voluntarily given up their time and money to help turn UKIP into a serious political force.

320PP PAPERBACK, £9.99

In an age of colourless bureaucrats, Nigel Farage is a politician who is impossible to ignore, provoking controversy and admiration in equal measure.

Never one for a quiet life, this edition includes the story of Nigel's extraordinary escape from death in a plane crash on the eve of the 2010 general election (the light aircraft he was flying in got caught up in a UKIP banner it was towing and crashed shortly after take-off, badly injuring Farage and his pilot), his recovery and return to the leadership of UKIP in November 2010.

Featuring sometimes hilarious and often terrifying encounters with a stellar supporting cast, including Tony Blair, Gordon Brown, Nicolas Sarkozy, José Manuel Barroso, and UKIP's short-lived, silver-gilt mascot, Robert Kilroy-Silk – and told with Farage's customary wit and humour – *Flying Free* is a candid, colourful life story by a fascinating and controversial character. It also shows that one fearless, determined individual can still make a difference.

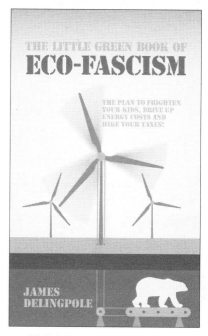